HALL of WATERS

BERRY GRASS

the operating system
KIN(D)* TEXTS & PROJECTS
print document

HALL OF WATERS

ISBN: 978-1-946031-54-9
Library of Congress Control Number: 2019947268
copyright © 2019 by Berry Grass
edited and designed by ELÆ [Lynne DeSilva-Johnson]

For additional questions regarding reproduction, quotation, or to request a pdf for review contact operator@theoperatingsystem.org

This text was set in Freight Neo, Minion Pro, and OCR-A Standard.

The cover art and cover font were created by Lynne DeSilva-Johnson [ELÆ], derived from the label of a souvenir 1956 glass bottle of mineral water, "Bottled by The Mineral Water System, Excelsior Springs, Missouri," bottled & sold at the Hall of Waters, courtesy of the author.

Books from The Operating System are distributed to the trade via Ingram, with additional production by Spencer Printing, in Honesdale, PA, in the USA.

The Operating System is a member of the **Radical Open Access Collective**, a community of scholar-led, not-for-profit presses, journals and other open access projects. Now consisting of 40 members, we promote a progressive vision for open publishing in the humanities and social sciences.

Learn more at: http://radicaloa.disruptivemedia.org.uk/about/

Your support makes our publications, platform and programs possible!
We <3 You.

the operating system
www.theoperatingsystem.org

HALL OF WATERS

Versions of these pieces first appeared in the following publications:

DONALD JUDD'S *UNTITLED (88-31 BERNSTEIN)*, *the tiny*
HALL OF WATERS; TO THE ARTIST DONALD JUDD...;
VICHEY GROUP IODIDE SPRING; AND DONALD JUDD'S
UNTITLED (STACK) MoMA, *The Wanderer*
REGENT SPRING, *Cherry Tree*
EXCELSIOR SPRINGS BOTTLING COMPANY, *Phoebe*
ACCOUNTABILITY 1; TRUE OR FALSE 1, *DIAGRAM*
DONALD JUDD'S *TO SUSAN BUCKWALTER*, The Fanzine
TRYST FALLS, *Shock of the Femme*
HISTORICAL SITE SURVEY--902 SUNSET STRIP, *Territory*
RELIEF SPRING, *smoke + mold*
HISTORICAL SITE SURVEY--30993 W 161ST ST, *Waxwing*

CONTENTS

Let's get to the point, like water does, rushing to fill all the spaces: this is about liquidity. What fills the spaces isn't whether or not I am your daughter but whether or not I can afford to be your daughter. There are costs involved. The empty spaces are what writing teachers call "place." It is understood by the writing teachers that place is the bodies of water where you are from. It is understood that a father's bottle of whiskey is itself a body of water. It is understood that until you surface, fluvial, in your womanhood there'll be empty spaces. So 1mg of liquid injected into the delta of my thigh every other week is getting to the point. Meanwhile the water levels everywhere else are rising, and that's getting to the point. The point is that this is about liquidity. What fills the spaces isn't whether or not a space can be defined in thought but whether or not I can afford the box. What fills the spaces isn't whether or not your many waters sustained me, Excelsior, but whether or not I can afford to live with your minerals in my blood. Am I obliged to your iron, am I in debt to your manganese. My alkaline inheritance.

HALL OF WATERS

Excelsior Springs, Missouri, was named an All-America City in 1974 by the National Civic League, and it truly is. My hometown, like so much of America, is the product of black labor and black intellect, taken by whiteness & celebrated like white achievement. Named for a poem by Henry Longfellow (himself a believer in white superiority), Excelsior was founded at the site of an iron manganese mineral water spring near Fishing River, in Clay County. Travis Mellion, a black farmer, discovered the spring's benefits—the water clearing up his daughter's scrofula, splashing away the king's evil—and was stamped out in the town records and the history classes by the doctors and pharmacists and charlatans who soon claimed the other springs in the area and built a health spa industry for politicians and Hollywood stars, until the spa's health claims were found to be bogus and the town dried up. Excelsior Springs grows more resentful each year of its shrinking population & fingertip-grip economy. It turns its resentment towards difference of all kinds: migrant labor, native persons, queer kids, anyone who isn't white. Its resentment is All-American. And it's such an easy metaphor: Springs/wells/ marginalizations. That what a place keeps underneath it is actually the thing that sustains it, makes it gush forward. But the truth is wells get used up and springs trickle to spit.

The Hall of Waters is an art deco masterpiece built with WPA money. Inside are curves of brass, thick lines of pale teal, and appropriated motifs of Mayan water gods. Serving today as City Hall, it was built around the site of that first spring. On the ground floor you can still visit the world's longest water bar, swill down the sulphur, gulp calcium, pretend you're better off for it. On the third floor is the municipal court, windows adjacent to the police station, where the rulings that uphold white supremacy daily sound out by gavel clap. And it's all so healthy, isn't it? So restorative? To soak in our nature's superior water and pretend that superiority is therefore our nature. To pretend that the concept of natural is natural.

There's a difference between hospitality and hospitable, much like there's a difference between a childhood and a survival. The tunnels and basements of the hotel, or the home, are where the living actually happens. I was a child and my biggest dream was to escape. *By which I mean*: in the Elms Hotel—the grand tourist business of Excelsior Springs, twice burned down, reinvented in old age as a venue for ghost tours—there was an escape chute. Al Capone had a private suite at the Elms. He would take the Wabash line train from Chicago to Excelsior to conduct liquor deals. In case of a police raid, the fireplace in his suite was actually a slide that brisked you down to the basement laundry room. You could slip out the maintenance door & lose the feds over at Regent Park.

My dad used to be head of maintenance at the Elms Hotel. He let me use Capone's chute and in my momentum I dreamed of escaping my father. I wanted to feel triumphant, like Harry S. Truman, who held up a newspaper—presidential election headline incorrectly stating "Dewey Defeats Truman"—on the Wabash line after staying at the Elms Hotel the night of the election. Truman ascended Democrat politics because he was backed by the corrupt Kansas City mob, and there's something here about Truman and Capone and crime and the inability to escape it all. *By which I mean*: I could slip my child's body out the back door of the Elms and, briefly, be rid of my dad & his abuse, but he would find me, probably by the old iron manganese spring a few yards south of The Elms, past the old Wabash train station, which is now the Wabash BBQ. And even if I wouldn't get caught there was still my mom & my brother back at home. An escape is never as clean as you'd like. You always leave something behind.

TO THE ARTIST DONALD JUDD, WHO FOUNDED AN ARTS COMMUNITY IN THE TOWN OF MARFA, IN THE VAST DESERT NOTHING OF WEST TEXAS, INSTEAD OF EVER RETURNING TO EXCELSIOR SPRINGS

I once told my mom that I was "probably the most famous person in town" just because I was once ranked 63rd in the United States at the Pokémon trading card game. I played the fool in that red Mercury Villager and I knew it. I knew that our town had college national track champions, had Major League Baseball players. The fame that people hope for their kids is athletic. It's all they know. My dad, my grandpa, they still wished for this kind of success for me, even after I was beaten for running like a girl, even after I was teased for reading girly books, even after I was on stage kissing a boy for all the town to see.

I hadn't heard of you yet, Donald. Nobody really speaks of you in Excelsior. Maybe it's because you got out. You got out & you only came back for quiet visits to your parents & grandparents & there is no memorial plaque hanging in the Hall of Waters, there is no installation of your work around town. There is no permanent gallery dedicated to you at the town museum, which is located in a decommissioned bank vault, which treats its own history like a privately held bond—you give up your history and it's never paid back to you. An exhibit of empty bottles & still thirsting for story. The athlete breaks down, becomes smaller, comes home, opens a shop. You went to the desert & your work scaled bigger. People visit Marfa now. There's a Prada store there. Excelsior Springs has one factory left & everyone buys their clothes at Wal-Mart or Goodys. Did you know if they resented you back home? Did any of this bother you?

To strip away from yourself the waters of youth, perhaps that was your intended minimalism. But you also took the horizon maw of the desert & partitioned it to boxes, smallnesses, like how Excelsior made you feel, and that was your minimalism too.

My maternal grandparents' house was a couple minutes northwest of Tryst Falls, a minor park feature, barely a waterfall, but oh that name, a Lover's Lane with the threat of drowning. That home was our coordinated rural escape, where dad wasn't welcome even when he wasn't drunk. We lusted after this safety then. I escape to black walnut trees, climb up & into myself. Grandpa's hunting dogs partitioned off and barking. The smell of gunpowder from the garage, where he filled shells while I read girly teen novels in secret. I learn to drive a tractor. How to fix a fence. I learn that sweet corn is best from a roadside stand and better than that from your own labor. This agricultural education does not feel confining, and all I want to do in summer is kiss cantaloupe, replace my body with loam & melonmusk. Tomatoes grow thick near the cattails and pond water, but back home mom's vines push pitiful, more fence-cling than anything, missing the plush and the burst. How you were raised is not the same way you should raise others.

DONALD JUDD'S *UNTITLED* (*88-31 BERNSTEIN*)
PRINCETON UNIVERSITY ART MUSEUM
PRINCETON, NEW JERSEY

Look at what's reflecting. My love, it's us beamed back from the gold rim of the box. Look at what's reflecting. My love, your parents don't know me at all and maybe I don't know me at all but you see us all on the side of the box anyway, next to each other. When a family stares at the same stack. When a reflection stretches & blurs. When no one says to any one why they aren't happy.

My friend Abbas and I have a goal to have one day pooped at all of the Ivy League schools. You're #3, Princeton. As if defecation could make humble all this gold gilt. Nothing about my body makes this place any more real to me. If I don't see a few river birch outside then I don't know how to fit in. New Jersey is a funhouse mirror. Donald, you're from where I'm from; no wonder your stack sees the same distortion.

There's a green plexiglass center within the seamless bounds of mirror. When mirror ends & box begins or does it. My love, how did you learn to see here and did it help you see plexiglass behind that beard I had in that moment, underneath that tarp of a tshirt? My love, two years since we visited Princeton with your parents (who still can't get my pronouns right), is what I am seeing in our bathroom mirror how I seem to you? Was it how I seemed back then, distorted? Look at what's reflecting.

Donald,

you wrote that: "good art

cannot contradict what is known

at the time it's made. If it does it's

just ignorant. Knowledge is knowledge

and art has to deal with that."

Good art is geocentric.

Good art is gendered via chromosome.

Good art says you're either autistic or trans,
     not both.

Good art has a small sample size.

Good art will measure the skulls of people, paint them

     into a caste system, paint them into a genre.

Good art gets government funding.

Good art is cited equally by eugenicists and Reddit memes.

Good art is studied systematically by white people.

Good art shows a possible link between caffeine and cancer.

Good art shows a possible link between abstaining

     from caffeine and cancer.

Good art kills your mother in an attempt to kill her

      cancer.

Good art is archivable, indexable.

Good art need not consent.

Good art has minerals.

Good art is for drinking.

Good art is found at the spa.

Good art will clear up your gout & cure your ulcer

      if you just swim in it.

Donald,

why did you sculpt boxes out in the high plains? Did you want to show that what we know is tiny? self-contained? sitting meek amidst the expanse of everything else? Somehow I don't think so. After all, is sculpture on Marfa land really different than a canvas hung on a white wall in New York? Is permanence worth the purchase? Do you even know?

The inpatient clients at the drug & alcohol rehab facility I worked for could do exactly three things outside of the building: 1.) they could walk two blocks down to church on Sundays, with employee supervison. 2.) They could stand on the side of the building, away from tourist traffic, to smoke. 3.) They could walk across that side street to sit at the old Vichey Iodide Spring. So much quiet reflection. I never found out what the Vichey Group was. One time a client brought me a fragment of an arrowhead he'd kicked up from the dirt near the spring. Did this town ever reflect on taking these springs from the Missouria & Osage people? White people in this town are addicted to meth & alcohol & monetizing what isn't theirs. This wet town on a wet hill. This town of colonized currents.

My father spent time at this center. It took him five 30-day stays before sobriety stuck. He found that higher power, one of those steps, I forget the number, I wasn't a counselor. All I did was care for the folks in social detox: give them a meal, make sure they're comfortable, talk with them through the comedown. People want a bed because that feeling of being clean will wash over them in 3 days or 30 days and they'll be a new person, but that's never how it really feels, even when you pass all 12 steps. Baptism. Baptism. Baptism. Baptism. I barely remember mine, age 13 at the old Methodist church, which used to be the new Methodist church, my eyes closed tight as a pour of water from a brass vessel slicked back my hair. That was it—no dunking, no bathing anew. I'd remember the same feeling a few years later, taking my pubescent body that wouldn't grow breasts out of the shower. I felt nothing.

THE SPACES

Siloam Spring. Regent Spring. Superior No.2 Spring. Steck's Iron Spring. Fowler's Magnaferro Spring. Crystal Lithium Spring. Excelsior Lithia Spring. Imperial Lithia Spring. Keystone Lithia Spring. Lithia No.1 Spring. Lithium Magnesium Spring. Montrose Spring. Peerless Spring. Old Smith Spring. Park Lithia Spring. Relief Spring. Soterian Spring. Willow Park Lithia Spring. Hiawatha Spring. Jones Soda Spring. Link Soda Spring. Muriated Soda Spring. Natrona Soda Spring. Pioneer Spring. Seltzer Salt Soda Spring. Soda Carbonic Spring. Soda Saline Spring. Sulphur Salt Soda Spring. Vichey Iodide Spring. Sulpho-Saline Spring. Salt Sea Spring. Salt Sulphur Spring. Salax Spring. Superior No.1 Spring. White Sulphur Spring. Sulpho-Saline Pavilion. Montezuma Pavilion. Sunnyside Spring.

"The waters are sold only in bottles bearing copyright labels; never in cans, jugs or kegs. They are bottled by a process which does not permit them to come in contact with the air from the time they leave the spring until the corks are pulled; all medicinal properties are therefore retained practically unchanged."

"Drink the water at regular intervals, if possible. Drink them slowly. Adopt, for the time at least, rational habits of eating, drinking and exercise. This will encourage the healing."

"A white attorney from Richmond, MO told a black farmer that the yellow water 'ought to be good for something' & suggested that he take some to give to his sick daughter, Opal, who was cured within weeks."

"Public restrooms were in high demand because of tourists buying bottles of sulpho-saline water, not knowing that it acts as a laxative."

"Settlers discovered these waters and their remedial uses."

"A single bottle contains 101mg/l of bone-building calcium, 25mg/l of cardio-strengthening magnesium, & 330mg/l of pH-balancing bicarbonates."

"Uncle Sam is buried in Excelsior Springs."

""She is curing more disease with her matchless
waters than any six health resorts put together in
the United States/It is estimated that thirty thousand
dollars are left in Excelsior Springs each week by our
prosperous visitors/And all this, has for its cause
or origin, the priceless virtues of Excelsior Springs
waters/"

Your furniture designs are being sold on a custom fabrication basis, Donald. This bed from 1979, for instance, costs between $12,500 and $29,250, depending on the choice of wood. It's only accessible on one side, being wrapped three quarters of the way around by pine (or cypress or black walnut or Douglass fir or or or). I can imagine your intent: to block out the rest of the room or the world from what happens in the sheets. To make the bed its own space to be present in. To clarify the essence of bedness, like if a bright spotlight could be something carved.

Enclosed on three sides by tall wood, imagine if you're on the inside, sleeping next to your abusive partner. Should their hands make a malicious turn on your body, your only escape from the bed would be through them. It's like casket practice. Donald, you once wrote about what distinguishes your furniture from your art, saying "if a chair or a building is not functional, if it appears to be only art, it is ridiculous." And I think about form and function. I think how a home like mine growing up was not broken or dysfunctional—it functioned nicely for abusive ends. I think about this bed, which is as much box as bed, and all my thoughts reduce down to this: you have never been a woman, Donald.

To take a shelf or table or chair and make a study of line and plane. To sell furniture for thousands of dollars. To saw lines so precise, so sharp, that the function of labor is entirely cut out. Your angles don't help the diapers get changed, your premium wood doesn't make the sex any better.

Not that the furniture in my house growing up was any better at facilitating reproductive labor. Your parents lived in Excelsior Springs until they passed away, and you hated the furniture in their house, which was probably a lot like ours. Donald, I'm really just trying to relate to you. I wish I could talk to you, but I can't, so I keep trying to find myself in you. I've left Excelsior too, Donald. I'm far away from the Midwest and I'm thinking about what it means to be an artist and I've read all your journals, and I keep reacting to your bluster and assuredness by finding fissures in your work. I find myself looking at your furniture trying to see the Midwest in it. If anything these designs reflect West Texas, that flat expanse, and not the Missouri hills where we both come from. Still, I'm trying to figure out why you left the Midwest and what you carried with you.

Still, I'm trying to figure out what kind of kitchen counters you'd make for my mom, what kind of cabinets you'd make for my Midwestern idyll: windows open, sun tea on the sill, oil crackling in the fryer, me and my mom dredging crappie filets through cornmeal, dancing together, Martina McBride on the stereo, dancing with each other like never before, making food for each other, dancing because we survived, dancing together as two women, a scene that I want to happen more than anything I've ever wanted, a scene that has never happened and never will. What kind of furniture has a funerary function. What kind of furniture looks like missing each other by months.

There's just a house with a trampoline out front now. They used to bottle enough water here to fill a train car every two days and now there's a house that looks like my old house. The Midwest is perhaps best defined as a place where domesticity is used as a cover-up. The first time I applied makeup to myself was when Mom taught me to use foundation and concealer to mask the bruise from my dad clutching my twig of an arm and tossing me into a wall. The Midwest is perhaps best defined as making the bed.

After the divorce, during our custody visits with him, Dad was frequently using meth. Having no practical ways to entertain or nurture his two kids, Dad would take us into the woods, up the large hills of Excelsior, to search for shiny somethings, to dig in the dirt. These pica weekends were spent searching for marbles, and Dad rattled off marble terminology, telling us how to separate agate marbles from mica marbles from End of Days marbles from glass marbles. He also had us looking for glass bottles. He was especially interested in local glass, from the Pepsi bottling plant which used to be here, or the mineral water plant which used to be here.

 And really I think of those days with my dad as his terrarium. In those days his ideas of the land & its history were preserved for him, and I was preserved for him in all of my potential to be the ideal small town Midwestern man that he once thought himself capable of being. Even now, breasts filled out and dusky rose lipstick applied, he still has this conception of a son he never had, as if he's keeping it under glass. Or maybe under agate, flecked with mica. I could never remember what he tried to teach me about marbles. I could never remember which materials reveal and which materials occlude. A pane of glass can be a false transparency, the scene lying beyond it staged, an artifice. The Midwest is perhaps best defined as a museum exhibit.

SULPHO-SALINE SPRING

"We're out all night/ Til broad daylight/ but we drink SULPHO saline in the morning" – from a print advertisement in which three owls stand on a bottle of Excelsior Springs Brewing Company water and sing

I was young when I realized I only want to worship where it's coming undone. I would walk in the woods and come across a circle of limestone. Rubbed smooth and worn with time, a cistern in the middle of it. You could tell there were eight stone piers around the cistern, a few stumps of which were still erect, and I imagined myself held in the palm of a powerful hand. I never felt any power in the pastel & stained glass of the Presbyterian church or the soft warm Methodist church where I was baptized. But here, at this abandoned well, I wanted to dance. There was just enough room on the slab to dance in a circle around the cistern and I imagined witches. I imagined chanting and song and reverence for this water.

Sulpho-saline water is a laxative. Some tourists to Excelsior Springs would only realize as much on the train leaving town, in a gurgling rush to the bathroom, after drinking at the Hall of Waters. The Excelsior Springs Bottling Company marketed this spring's waters as "a morning bracer for the club-man," which can relieve your hangover symptoms. Print advertisements also claimed, almost entirely erroneously, that sulpho-saline water treats or even cures "jaundice, galls stones [sic], constipation; diseases of the rectum, hemorrhoids, etc; catarrhal conditions of the nasal passages, throat, stomach, and intestines; dyspepsia, acidity and flatulency of the stomach; headache; all diseases of the skin."

If you can believe that. Faith is a kind of evacuation, and the problem with church was that upon emptying myself the spirit did not rush in to replace me. I was asked to refuse myself for the sake of transformation, but I remained empty. No song, no hymn would move me except that of cricket, of creek, an abandoned shelter taken over by moss, by spiders, of a sudden cistern, of sunlight warming the green ground, of a doe in the distance, of green of green of green of green.

Donald, this is my favorite of your plexiglass stacks. Twelve shelves sitting hydroponic green, vertical, as if every front lawn in my neighborhood growing up together made a ladder leading to nothing. I see this green & I see nature, hear Fishing River trickling, smell my mom's overgrown garden. You saw this green & saw industry, motorcycle lacquer, the sheen of bass boats, you saw production. You thought nature inert until you complicated it with a few boxes. You wrote that "the box is a neutral form, that it has no symbolic meaning." But I look at your stack, green as grass as my last name as the confines of family, and all I see is symbol. All I see in every box is a symbol I stand in. People deny my personhood because I am just a symbol. I stand waiting in line for the bathroom and I am just a symbol. I stand out in public and I am green, I am a monster. I move from room to room, each identity a box, the more boxes the more I am a monster. What we mean when we say monster is "symbol." What we mean when we say boxes is "confine the monster." Donald, you wrote that "actual space is intrinsically more powerful and specific than paint on a flat surface." But you never quite got there —two-dimensional canvas or three-dimensional box, your use of space is still symbolic because it is boxes, boxes all the way down. I want to know: What is actual space when you are a monster? What if actual space was more than where I am stacked standing?

MISSOURI DEPARTMENT OF NATURAL RESOURCES
STATE HISTORIC PRESERVATION OFFICE, P.O. Box 176,
Jefferson City, MO 65102

ARCHITECTURAL/HISTORIC INVENTORY FORM

1. Survey No. CL-AS-7-18	2. Survey name: Excelsior Springs Historic Resources	
3. County: Clay	4. Address (Street No.) 902	Street (name) Sunset Strip

5.City: Excelsior Springs	Vicinity: ☐	6. Geographical Reference: 39.358275, -94.229861	7. Township/Range/Section: T: 52N R: 30W S:1

8.Historic name (if known): Grass Residence; Garden House; Connie's House; The One With The Birdfeeders; Twice-Yearly Garage Sale; Flamingo Flock; Connie's Bar & Grill	9. Present/other name (if known): It's not Connie's anymore.

10. Ownership: ☒ Private ☐Public	11a. Historic use (if known): Horror and refuge. It was wet with booze breath & then verdant with rootgrowth. Less desperate than it was. Decorated.	11b. Current use: Unknown. After mom passed the property changed owners, an unfamiliar red truck visible in the driveway on Google Maps, renovated with white shiplap, all the music taken out of it.

HISTORICAL INFORMATION

12. Construction date: 1971	15. Architect: n/a	18. Previously surveyed? ☐ Cite survey name in box 22 cont. (page 3)
13. Significant date/period: 1992-2016	16. Builder/contractor: n/a	19. On National Register? ☐ individual ☐ district Cite nomination name in box 22 cont. (page 3)
14. Area(s) of significance: AGRICULTURE; HEALTH/MEDICINE; LAW	17. Original or significant owner: Connie Grass	20. National Register eligible? ☐ individually eligible ☐ district potential ☐ not eligible ☒ not determined

ARCHITECTURAL/HISTORIC INVENTORY FORM

21. History and significance on continuation page. ☒	22. Sources of information on continuation page. ☒

ARCHITECTURAL INFORMATION

23. Category of property: ☐ building(s) ☒ site ☐ structure ☐ object	30: Roof material: Asphalt shingle	37.Windows: ☐ historic ☒ replacement Pane arrangement:
24. Vernacular or property type:	31. Chimney placement: Offset left	38. Acreage (rural): Visible from public road? ☐
25. Architectural Style: Split-level Ranch style	32. Structural system: Wood frame	39. Changes (describe in box 41 cont.): ☐ Addition(s) Date(s):
26. Plan shape: Rectangular	33. Exterior wall cladding: Brick and lumber	☐ Altered Date(s): ☐ Moved Date(s):
27. No. of stories: 1 Front 2	34. Foundation material: Unknown	☐Other Date(s): Endangered by: Drought. Flood.
28. No. of bays (1st floor): Seven	35. Basement type: Full	40. No. of outbuildings (describe in box 40 cont.):
29. Roof type: Truncated Hip	36. Front porch type/placement: Platform	41. Further description of building features and associated resources on continuation page. ☒

OTHER

42. Current owner/address: [Redacted]	43.Form prepared by (name and org.): [the woman who had a gross boyhood here, with a name that no longer fits]	44. Survey date: 2018
		45. Date of revisions:

ARCHITECTURAL/HISTORIC INVENTORY FORM

FOR SHPO USE

Date entered in inventory:	Level of survey	Additional research needed?
	☐ reconnaissance ☒ intensive	☒ yes ☐ no
National Register Status: ☐ listed ☐ in listed district Name: ☐ pending listing ☐ eligible (individually) ☐ eligible (district) ☐ not eligible ☐ not determined	Other:	

LOCATION MAP (include north arrow)
PHOTOGRAPH (taken Oct. 2013)

LOCATION

ARCHITECTURAL/HISTORIC INVENTORY FORM

PHOTOGRAPH

Photographer:	Date:	Description:
Google Street View	Oct. 2013	Fall color masks the state of browning, the wilting walls of plants cradling every post, a long makeshift fence of bushes, nothing upright without plants encircling its base.

ADDITIONAL INFORMATION:

21. (cont.) History and significance. Expand box as necessary, or add continuation pages.

Because to voice the desire to escape would only bring his fist. Desire disturbs the air in the house, thickens the place like roux, and dad would swat and swat as if clearing smoke. In the Midwest we value the Privacy of the Domestic Sphere. "Adults can do whatever they want as long as they keep it in the privacy of their own bedroom," say all of the good men and women in town, over their shoulders to their children, at even the slightest hint of queerness. They lump queerness in with the actual perils they allow the home to cover up: the screaming, the recycling full of aluminum cans, the shattered plates, the craters in the drywall.

The significance of this house is the lesson that nothing private stays. You can only live in town for so long before other people's parents hear about your dad's drinking. You can only go to school for so long before people begin to wonder about the bruises. Life in the rural Midwest is a timeline of when private experiences are made public. Only your internality can escape.

We moved into 902 Sunset Strip from a castle-gray box on N. Kimball because my parents wanted more room for me & my brother. Or maybe just for herself. My mom painted the front room clay-orange & hung southwestern landscapes on the walls. And what she meant to say to me, to everyone in the house, even my dad, every neighbor that visited, what she meant by this was: *I have been depleted by this man and this life but I will raise these children and I will teach my students. I want more than what I have. I am emptied but I am vast.* And when the orange gave way to peapod green, she was speaking to us again: *I will outlive you because unlike you, there is bloom in me yet.*

In the years after the divorce, my mom would begin to plant shrubs and perennials and tomatoes and big blossoms around the entire perimeter of the property, lining every bit of fence with something green. And I know she was making friends on music message boards. And I know from reading her journals after she passed away that she was dating. And I know that her reputation was turning around from "the teacher with the awful husband" and "the woman who runs the best garage sale in town" to "the wild plant lady." But this was speech, unvoiced. Seeds planted and soil nurtured and speech harvested. She was trying to tell us that she was growing.

By the time she told me about her cancer diagnosis, the front room and

the bedroom and the kitchen had taken on a beach theme. New England
shore kitsch lined the shelves in the kitchen and the other rooms were
inspired by Floridian aesthetics. We never talked about how scared she was,
or how she felt about dying. But she was telling me something by
manifesting shell and seaspray around her. She was saying: *This is where I
hope to be soon, one way or another. On the edge of worlds and, with
politeness towards the waves, finally, taken in.*

40. (cont.) Description of environment and outbuildings. Expand box as
necessary, or add continuation pages.

    Home located in a late-1960s or early-1970s subdivision on the
westernmost part of town. This subdivision, not formally named, was built
around Peachtree Street, Dogwood Street, Apple Blossom Street, Michele
Street, Milwaukee Street, and Miss Belle Street. It was intended to be a more
affordable neighborhood compared to the more deluxe planned subdivision
in western Excelsior Springs, King's Edition, which was next to the hospital.
Home is located near the Canadian Pacific Railway line, which ran through
thick forest that could take you all the way to Salem Road, past city limits.
The train would shake the walls of the house and the Jewel tea dishes would
rattle and it was a reminder that it was possible to move forward, to leave.
Home had consistent yellow paint with blue trim.

    Home was in the middle of a short block of three homes total; Connie
Grass had made a de-facto fence for the front-facing side of the property by
planting a wide variety of plants along each property line; a deliberate
differentiation from the well-kept lawns and lack of front fencing in the rest of
the neighborhood. It is unclear whether the plants were there for her
protection or for the protection of her neighbors.

41. (cont.) Description of primary resource. Expand box as necessary, or add
continuation pages.

    The bedroom of the oldest child was sky blue for a number of years,
but was painted black during their adolescence. After moving out, it became
a peach-hued museum hosting Connie's collection of concert photos and
musician's autographs. Its final stage was a Thomas the Tank Engine-
themed room for Connie's grandson.

    The basement, nominally a recreation room, was a mixture of lime
green paint and wood paneling. The music museum took its place down here
when Connie's youngest child had a son. The museum expanded. The front
room and kitchen first took on an American southwest/*Arizona Highways*
feel, with sandy colored walls and framed images of buttes and mesas. It
would, as if a drought reversed, become greener and greener over the years,

as plants and framed pictures of Anne Geddes' photography replaced the more arid decorations. Its final stage was an embrace of Florida Keys chic: seashore village romanticism and Margaritaville-style resort town aesthetics. The garage was never used to store vehicles. It hosted garage sales once, sometimes twice a year, for necessary supplemental income. Connie would try to sell any and every toy or shirt that wasn't getting frequent use. If the contents of the home are self-expression, the garage served as a way to store expressive acts that no longer served a use. A warehouse of discarded desire.

The present occupants of the home have painted every room white and gray-mauve. White shiplap blankets the entryway and kitchen. New faux-marble countertops and quaint "country" fixtures adorn the kitchen. Everything looks as if draped by the veil of a ghost.

Sodium toxicity results in the shrinking of cellular tissues, especially

in the brain and lungs, causing cellular paralysis.

Lithium toxicity results in renal failure, severe cognitive

impairment, seizures

Iodine toxicity results in dermal ulcers, a constant metallic taste

coating your mouth & tongue—like something is wrong

and you haven't yet realized that what's wrong is

you're not what they say you are, and

hyperthyroidism

Iron toxicity results in abdominal pain, vomiting, diarrhea, then

a curious pause in which you think things are getting better

before you experience seizures, liver failure,

and glycemic failure

Nitrite toxicity results in the over production of hemoglobin, which

is to say it sends more iron all throughout your body.

Which is to say just because someone doesn't abuse

you directly doesn't mean they didn't

contribute to your abuse, amplify it,

send it brainward

Nitrate toxicity results in the body's inability to carry

    oxygen in the blood

Manganese toxicity results in erratic motor skills impairment,

    depersonalization, dissociation, loss of sense of self

Potassium toxicity results in cardiac arrhythmia & eventual

    cardiac arrest.

Sulphur toxicity results in aggravation of bronchial-respiratory

    distress & pulmonary dysfunction. Not classified as

        especially dangerous, it is most experienced

            in toxic amounts as a restriction of the

                airway, as a microaggression, a gas

                    set to sweep past the box

                        of lit matches you

                            carry inside

                                you.

You understand my meaning, Excelsior. There is nothing to drink here. You have nothing to offer me. You understand my metaphor, Excelsior. How I tried to filter

    all of this

                                     out.

In the purified water industry they call the filtering process "reverse osmosis" and we both understand this, Excelsior. We both understand how I carry your toxicity with me, how I picked it up without knowing what I was swallowing. You handed me a glass of water. It was cold. So what if it smelled like sewer eggs, so what if it was occluded. You said it was cold. You said it was pure.

I will try to speak plainly of the violence of indigenous erasure. Nearly every piece of written history about Excelsior Springs mentions that Travis Mellion discovered the first waters, at what would be called Siloam Spring. Any mention of indigenous peoples using the waters prior to 1880 is typically characterized as use by "prehistoric Indians," referring to what archeologists call the Nebo Hill civilization of 3,000-1,000 BCE. I will try to speak plainly: the idea that nobody used these waters from 1,000 BCE to 1880 CE, nearly 3,000 years, is audacious. This settler town swigging down fictions, drinking deeply of words like "discovery."

The only significant written source I've ever found that acknowledges an indigenous presence in even the few hundred years before Excelsior's founding is a self-published book from 1940 by Dr. Aretus S. McCleary. Aretus was the founder and head doctor at the McCleary Sanitarium and Clinic, and his book was presented as the history of native safekeeping around Excelsior Springs, which was then known among tribes as Peace Valley. The title of the book is *The Legend of Peace Valley: told by Wapoo, Keeper of the Springs*. The hardback cover simply read WAPOO, with an embossed logo of an indigenous stereotype in the bottom right corner. The title page mentions that "This is the story of how Wapoo, an Indian hunter, discovered the mineral springs now known as Excelsior Springs, in the ages long before white men set foot in the valley" and that's the last full quote from this book that I will share because all of it is a lie. Wapoo—a caricature of indigenous wisdom—is an invention of McCleary's. Wapoo says that Peace Valley was known continent-wide, that all the tribes knew about the healing waters at Echo Canyon (later to be known as Siloam Spring). Nobody called that creek Echo Canyon. Nobody called the area Peace Valley. These waters were not known across all of Turtle Island as a place of restoration. None of the prose or the verse in this book, none of the photographs, depict anything real at all. This is the only significant written history of Excelsior Springs to mention modern indigeneity, and it does so only to craft a settler fantasy to sell spa treatments.

FOWLER'S MAGNAFERRO SPRING

"The water is very rich in iron but is not as 'hard' as water from the other springs, which will give it a decided advantage to invalids with delicate stomachs. It is of undoubted medicinal value."

Infants cannot purge manganese. It is understood by the clinicians and the pediatricians that while manganese is a trace element essential to normal body function, too much manganese will stick to the frothed fat of a child's brain.

You can see two churches from the site of the old Fowler's Inn. Over the rooftops there's Christ Our Redeemer Church, where I once saw a neighbor kid get baptized in a slender tub washed over in bottle-green window light after a day of religious summer school. Catty-corner from the Inn is an old church building now housing the Slightly Off Broadway community theater. And really, what's the difference. A community will tell itself stories about its values & histories. A sermon is in some ways a soliloquy. And the stories are meant to stick. A large community church gathering and the re-staging of a play after its original run in a community has concluded are both called a revival.

William Ellsworth Fowler owned the inn & the iron manganese well he called Fowler's Magnaferro Spring. He was a lawyer, probate judge, & presidential Elector. He was more popularly known around town as a poet. Stashed in a box in our garage growing up, there was a framed diptych of a picture of a United States flag & a poem by Fowler titled "The Call of the Flag." Written preceding the United States' involvement in World War I, the poem is about one's patriotic duty to shed blood for one's country. I saw this same diptych at dozens of garage sales growing up, being sold for pennies by people who were young adults during the Vietnam War. I imagine hundreds more in town still collecting dust on old walls. You can give away the stories you don't want anymore, but all that means is that someone else has them.

In the January 1907 issue of *Watson's Jeffersonian Magazine* (an issue in which the editor writes in favor of dismissal of African-American troops & in favor of segregating "children of Mongolian descent"—by which he ignorantly referred to Japanese ethnicity), Fowler published a poem titled "You Old Confeds." It's a schlocky paean to fallen Confederate soldiers and the Righteousness of their cause. He was a lawyer & a probate judge & a presidential Elector & a poet & owned his Inn & owned his Magnaferro Spring & these are all connected. Who you welcome to stay with you, who you nourish, who is celebrated in your art, who sits in judgment of your own gavels. Your access to power. Your proximity to and participation in whiteness. It's inseparable from the art.

Just one block away is Broadway Avenue, running past the diner, the museum, the green yard of the Hall of Waters. Every summer the Waterfest Parade route comes through here & there are tents & treats & vendors. In 2018, the Excelsior Springs Chamber of Commerce approved as a vendor the "2nd Missouri Militia" Sons of Confederate Veterans group. They were allowed to sell Confederate/Tennessee/Virginia battle flags & flag shirts & flag bumper stickers & bumper stickers with racist phrases. The ensuing discussion on a town Facebook group was full of open white supremacy and denial of the realities of chattel slavery. Everyone making sure that their stance is recorded for posterity. Facebook being the same thing as a congregation or a community theater. Facebook being a performance, the stories that a community tells itself. It's 2019 and there's a revival in Excelsior Springs. The story under the tent is the same as it always was.

DOXEY BATH HOUSE

And you're never taught that Excelsior had a Jim Crow school across the street from where a one-pagoda, one-swingset park now stands. Like many segregated schools in the Missouri River Valley, it was called Lincoln School. The park itself is called Lincoln Park, and there is no historical marker making mention of Lincoln School, despite the building still standing, now a private residence. And you're never taught that African Americans were barred from all city parks in Excelsior Springs. Early Sanborn maps of the town leave off Lincoln School, despite it being established in 1888 as Excelsior's second ever school. And what's really learned when things are erased, painted over, pages torn out? Herbert Elett, a former Lincoln School student, described his education there like this: "It's like this—one page may have 'little boy blue come blow your horn,' you'd turn the page and the rest of the story wouldn't be there—we never got the whole story."

And you're never taught that the Colored Baptist Church might have been the first church building in Excelsior Springs. Early maps left off that church too. And while schools take you on field trips to The Elms Hotel, and while everybody knows that the old Oaks Hotel is down the street from the Hall of Waters, you're never taught that The Albany Hotel was where Black tourists and Black workers stayed, and you're never taught that The Albany Hotel existed at all. And you're never taught that Excelsior Springs had a Negro Business League—thought to be the very first in the state of Missouri. And you're never taught that the secretary of Excelsior's Negro Business League, W.A. Doxey, founded his own bath house.

And you're never taught that W.A. Doxey and his wife, Katie, were specially trained in Swedish massage technique and also in administering the Betz hot air treatment. And you're never taught that the Doxey Bath House served Black clients as well as white ones. And you're never taught that Dr. D.A. Ellet came from Howard University's medical school to practice medicine in Excelsior Springs in 1888, and that he opened up Star Bath House after managing the spa at The Elms Hotel. And you're never taught that the very first bath house operator in Excelsior, Robert Spence Ewing, was Black. Their contributions to the growth of Excelsior Springs torn out of the town's popular narratives. Black people, from farmhands to physicians, understood the waters and their vapors. And you're never taught the whole story.

Boxes like epochs, Donald, I keep trying to divide your biography into proportions clean & neat as the lines in your work. I keep trying to see Excelsior run through it all, the river of your life, as if a river is ever anything else than life.

You hadn't thought to stack them yet, Donald. This was when you first hung boxes on the wall: four galvanized iron boxes placed six inches apart horizontally; a single blue beam, aluminum, laid on top of them like a rolled wave tumbling through the white space & the shine & the gleam and I know you distrusted allusion in art but this looks like a timeline. Chronology is the art of boxing in our lives, the art of narrative, and I could say plenty here about Didion & telling ourselves stories in order to live, but I'd rather think about being galvanized. You galvanize iron by layering over it a protective coating of zinc. When they thought I was a boy I was shiny, reflective. When they thought I was a boy I was a wilderness with a wrong map. And the whole time I thought *when there's drought in the river we still call it a river, so why don't you see me as what I am?* Each of us can hold at once that I was both me and not me, or that to galvanize is to craft a shell for saving but to galvanize is to spark a muscle to action, and it's always both: the hiding and the coming out.

Nobody seems to know what year this piece is from. Most sources say 1964, but I've seen '65 and even '69 cited. Nobody seems to know what year I am from. I mean, what year are any queers from? When is the queer birth, the coming out or the coming into, when my partner first touched me or when I first touched her, the ancestral lineage of touch, years of yearning stitched back through time like she and I are yarn & have been this whole time, like we're filigree. Or like a rolling blue spine but all they see is boxes. I'm trying to make a narrative again aren't I but the fact of my body together with the fact of her body is making something else, something gently held, and you didn't understand that disruption has an eros, Donald. You only touched what you wished kept away from others. And I know you distrusted allusion in art but your boxes have always been full of storage.

ENRICHMENT

You have likely consumed the water of Excelsior Springs. A 2013 study of the water footprint in large-scale pasta production indicates that for every kilogram of dry pasta manufactured, about 1.3-2.1 liters of water are used. Excelsior Springs was chosen in 1988 for American Italian Pasta Company's new plant—still the largest pasta production facility in North America—because of its abundance of fresh spring water. By 1991 their mission to "make the best pasta in the country" had shifted to low-cost pasta, to cornering market share.

[Water wasted/ rinsed through/ a treatment.]

The legacy of these waters is in every bite. 350 million pounds worth, distributed throughout the U.S. each year. But it's a fallacy to think that settler prejudices are part of a unique mineral composition. Excelsior is not the source of these turgid things. The entire Midwest, the entire country, perpetuates these ideas. Excelsior is not unique in this way. Believe me when I tell you that I am not writing these essays because Excelsior Springs is unique. I'm writing these essays because water will be our creator and our undoing, because the entire region and the entire political body is complicit. Your town has its own histories, its own fraudulent spas. Your town manufactures marginalization too.

[Water wasted/ rinsed through/ a treatment]

"Here the air is pure and bracing, there is no malaria, there are no mosquitoes, and cool, health-giving, life-saving springs are seen; here peace and quietness is found, health restored, the invalid becomes well again, and those who seek a quiet place to rest and build up, rejoice in finding such a beautiful resort."

"Excelsior Springs is one of the most metropolitan cities for its size in the United States."

"Among the laxative waters, sulpho-saline stands alone—without peer…It is mild and sure in its action. It never gripes."

"There is evidence of peoples occupying the land in the area for almost 7,000 years prior to white settlement."

"The water purportedly had remarkable properties: if a metal utensil was sunk into the basin overnight, it gained magnetic properties and could pick up a small object."

"Powerful as the waters are, it is the opportunities offered the visitor to get close to nature without undergoing hardships that really quicken and tone the sluggish muscle and add grace and youthful snap to the movement of aging bodies."

"Excelsior Springs water contains
protocarbonate of iron in solution, a
constituent of the blood, and one that is
absent in alcoholism. These waters supply this
constituent with abundance, and by itstonic
effect upon the brain and nerve tissues of
the body, the craving for stimulants is less
pressing."

"There is not such a group or variety of mineral springs on
the globe, as exist here. We have the laxative, the ant-acid, the
lithiated, and the ferruginous ...Where in any locality ...could
you find the waters of any six well-known health resorts together
that would make a combination equal to ours?"

It's so easy to pave over your shame in the Midwest. To take your history and flatten it out. Queers in the Midwest know this keenly. Two centuries of "he's just your Uncle's good friend" and "she's just always been a tomboy" and "he used to wear dresses from time to time but he grew some sense." Two settler centuries here of pretending queers don't exist, and when they can't pretend anymore? A closet of contusions.

Which is to say: c'mon, this was a *bathhouse*. Shared steam rooms and private hotel beds on site. Men were fucking each other in Excelsior Springs. Men have always fucked each other in the Midwest, and they certainly were fucking each other at the Montezuma Bath House. Men were certainly driving in from across the region to "partake of the waters." Men were taking the Wabash line down from Chicago for a bit of rest and relaxation and a few handsome strangers to drink in. Women, too, were being very good friends with each other in the discreet spas of Excelsior Springs. Sheets soaked, stained. Voices crying out from that *good* cure.

I do not have historical record of this. The Midwest does not record that which it prefers go unacknowledged. But c'mon. I wasn't born yesterday, and neither were you, and neither were other queer people. Like most spaces in the Midwest that queers made a world out of, Montezuma's Bath House was only in operation for a few years. Same with Powell's Bath House and Royal Bath House and Star Bath House and Electric Bath House and Harris Bath House and Siloam Bath House and Knox Bath House and Kihlberg's Karlsbad Bath House and Doxey Bath House and Battle Creek Bath House. Two, three, ten years at the most, before some moneyed interest came to buy out the real estate & spring access, to build a pagoda or a pharmacy. The Montezuma became the main building for the Ball Clinic—the health facility most associated with Excelsior Springs' health industry and with the town's economic decline after fraudulent health claims were exposed. Now, the whole building is gone. A parking lot took its place. And it's what happens to queer spaces across the Midwest: they close, and what replaces them closes, and in the historical record it won't even be marked as a disappearance. In true Midwestern form, it's like they never even existed in the first place.

SUPERIOR SPRING

"All water is diuretic but Superior is distinctly so. . . By systematic use of the Superior, with other waters, crutches will be laid aside and the step becomes elastic."

It's amazing the things people confuse for something else. A trademarked treatment for a healing. A pulpit politics for a lesson. Superior Spring is actually two wells less than a block away from each other. It's said that Superior No.1 was a sulpho-saline spring and Superior No.2 was an iron manganese spring. Superior Spring has the last remaining extant pagoda structure in Excelsior Springs, but residents are often confused if the pagoda houses Superior No.1 or Superior No.2. There are maps that confirm which is which but some folks need more than that—need a water purity test or an oral history. Some folks aren't prepared to accept a true answer about things, about anything really, and maybe this is what makes Excelsior Springs a Missouri town.

The generalization is that Missourians walk through life with a healthy dose of skepticism and a thirst for proof. "You've got to show me" is the unofficial state motto (the actual motto being *Salus populi suprema lex esto*—"The welfare of the people shall be the supreme law"). It's found on shirts and bumper stickers and the nickname itself—The Show-Me State—is on the state license plate. The website for the Missouri Secretary of State's office offers a brief explanation for the phrase. The story goes that in 1899, Missouri Congressman Willard Duncan Vandiver was arguing in Philadelphia over some Naval Affairs business. Vandiver gave a rebuttal that earned his state some national respect when he said: "I come from a state that raises corn and cotton and cockleburs and Democrats, and frothy eloquence neither convinces nor satisfies me. I am from Missouri. You have got to show me."

Another, less flattering, origin of the phrase comes from the mines of Colorado in the mid-1890's, where foremen replaced the miners that were on strike with scabs from other states. Because supposedly the scab miners from Missouri were too inept or inexperienced for the job, the common phrase when a scab miner was receiving instructions was "This man is from Missouri. You'll have to show him."

There's no proof for either of the stories behind "The Show-Me State." Missouri doesn't actually want the truth. It wants to demand a proof that feels right. It wants to be told that it's right, not shown how it's in the wrong.

It makes me doubt what I'm doing here, writing this book, because I am trying to show the town proof of its history. I am trying to show how all of us who grew up there, even those of us used up & cast out, are settlers, complicit. I am trying to show how very typically Midwestern we are. But to be shown something is not the same thing as *seeing* it, and I worry that Excelsior Springs won't see this book. I worry that my act of showing will be confused for an act of betrayal, a declaration of hatred, for the place and its people.

I'd like to show other people the walking trail around Watkins Mill. I'd like to show people how to fish for crappie, the sun glinting off of a bright lure. I'd like to show other people the old tiles in the lobby of the Elms hotel, or the art-deco lines in the Hall of Waters. I'd like to show people the lunch counter at Ray's, treat them to a hamburger. I'd like to show people a patch of morels in the good good dirt. I'd like to show people the seats I saw the '94 and '96 ESHS Tigers state championship football teams from. I'd like to show people the steam rising off of a cup of hot chocolate behind the bleachers on a Friday night. I'd like to show people the ways that a church community comes together for a member of its congregation in need. I'd like to show people fireworks, a barbecue competition, a fried tenderloin sandwich, a drive down Isley Boulevard & out down 10 Highway, up the big hill, into a Ray County sunrise. I'd like to show people what you're so proud of, Excelsior. The things that I miss about you, the things I recognize myself in. But it's hard for me to do that when you won't let those things be seen by people who aren't like you.

When your bed & breakfast is named after & located in an old jail. When your pastors reach out to trans people to dissuade them from transitioning. When you use the phrase "Job Corps kid" as a routine dogwhistle for racial slurs. When your school board refuses to let the high school perform plays about race or queerness. When whiteness builds up on you like decades of calcium deposits. When your whiteness is a refusal, a private pagoda.

The word "Excelsior" is often translated from Latin as "ever upward." The word Excelsior is a superlative that the town has long stopped trying to live up to. It's imperative that I always see that. That all superiority is false is a refusal to see when shown.

·

DONALD JUDD'S *UNTITLED (COPPER)*,
TATE MODERN,
LONDON, ENGLAND

There's no equation for the way time extends itself, reaching, while you stand in front of the barrel of a gun. One second passes, your dad's finger hesitating over the trigger, all breath suspended, one more second passes and still he's there, back to the hallway closet he pulled the rifle out of and still you're there, back up against your mom, her back up against the screen door, your baby brother in her right arm, each second seeming longer than the one before it. It feels like mere seconds ago that you were thrown up against the wall in your bedroom & now you're backing up to the door and your dad is going to shoot you all.

We lived, clearly, or I wouldn't be thinking of that night as I look at this 1973 copper sculpture of yours. It's trying so hard to be perfectly, mathematically beautiful that it winds up with ugly evocations. Buffed and polished roundnesses, a logical proof, a penny trigonometry. Four bullnose projections extending towards the viewer as half-orbs from the central copper beam. Each circular slickness increasingly wider than the one before it, 1.5 inches wider each time, with the space between the projections simultaneously decreasing by 1.5 inches as the piece moves left to right. I think about seconds feeling longer at the same time as your life shortens. I think about how any personal growth you do (I do, my dad does, anyone) comes at the cost of time to spend while grown.

I think about how art needs a viewer to activate. This sculpture, its mechanical cradle, is a rifle's chamber waiting for a viewer, me, to be its bolt. In a bolt action rifle, you pull out the bolt to expose a cavity in the chamber into which you place your bullet. When you push the bolt back in, that bullet is guided into place for firing. I look at this sculpture, gleaming with violent potential. It looks like the bullet. It looks like the chamber. It looks like a sequence of exit wounds, a time-lapse of a bullet moving through walls, a brief history recorded in holes.

The only imperfection in this piece, the only crack in the math, is an inscription found at the back of the sculpture, out of sight. It reads "72-21 JO" and I've come to learn this about you, Donald, that you give credit to others in whispers. This is a record of the sculpture's making. Your 21st fabrication order in 1972. "JO" stands for José Otero, the worker at Bernstein Bros. metalworking facility in Long Island. The man who actually made this sculpture. It's your design, sure, your math. But Otero fabricated your pieces for you. And while there's nothing novel in the history of art about outsourcing the labor of its manufacture, I'm thinking about the particular violence of erasure.

Your works are celebrated for how they dissolve their ideas into the impersonal. Like you've created new Platonic forms, essential shapes. I think you appreciated how the industrial fabrication process is perfect in a way that an artist's brushstroke or chiselstrike cannot be. How it took your body out of the work. I've read your journals, Donald. I don't have José's writing, so I can't know how he felt about being alienated from his labor. While your outsourcing sought to eliminate you from your work, I can't know how José felt about being invisible to begin with.

Some twenty five years after your death now and your fabrication of Marfa, Texas as an arts town has eliminated Marfa, Texas the cattle town from the story of Marfa, Texas. A history of ranchers and freight trains. And that's just the settler history—what of the indigenous peoples of West Texas, invisible? What of the La Junta peoples? The Apache? The Comanche? Marfa's arts infrastructure was made possible by imperialism. You bought the old military buildings of Fort D.A. Russell and made great sculpture halls, artist residencies, open-air galleries. Today the space is neighboring a U.S. Border Patrol outpost. I wonder where you would have made this place if you hadn't passed through West Texas on an army bus, en route to Los Angeles, where you then shipped out as an engineer to American horrors of the Korean War. Which place, whose story, would you have your shadow fabricated onto if your bus had taken a different route?

Ugly evocations: what a gun can get you. Ugly evocations: working only from a design given to you. My dad did not fire the rifle at us, perhaps only because my mom fled out the front door, my brother in her arms, me following, across the yard & behind a neighbor's truck parked on the street. I can never shake out the memory, but I've come to doubt my dad's sincerity that night. He was merely fabricating that violence, I think. When his body reached for that gun and pressed the stock into the soft give of his shoulder, I think he was only acting out a misogynist design handed out to him. A Midwestern schematic that says your wife is disposable, and your little boy that's too much like a girl is too much like disposable. The violence done was not created so much as it was already there, waiting to be activated.

MISSOURI DEPARTMENT OF NATURAL RESOURCES
STATE HISTORIC PRESERVATION OFFICE, P.O. Box 176,
Jefferson City, MO 65102

ARCHITECTURAL/HISTORIC INVENTORY FORM

1. Survey No. RY-AS-11-18	2. Survey name: Excelsior Springs Historic Resources		
3. County: Ray	4. Address (Street No.) 30993	Street (name) W 161st St	
5.City: Excelsior Springs	Vicinity: X	6. Geographical Reference: 39.384720, - 94.20584	7.Township/Range/Section: T: 53N R: 29W S:19
8.Historic name (if known): Grandma & Grandpa's house. Black velvet house. Antler velvet house. Fortress house. Escape house.		9. Present/other name (if known): I don't and likely never will know.	
10. Ownership: X Private ☐ Public	11a. Historic use (if known): Cantaloupe, mostly. The melons and tomatoes and okra grown here: oh let there be a record. Let there be a record of strung- up bucks in the garage, of flank and chuck, of bloodletting, steamy, down the garage drain. Please record, too, the history of hiding from drunk fathers. Let there be a record of refuge. Let there be a record of guns.	11b. Current use: Maybe it's still an escape, just someone else's escape. My brother and I had to sell the property after our mom passed away. An isolated, rural home we couldn't afford to live in. Maybe the trees are still fruiting. Maybe the soil still yields. Maybe it doesn't matter that I don't know.	

HISTORICAL INFORMATION

12. Construction date: 1974	15. Architect: n/a	18. Previously surveyed? ☐ Cite survey name in box 22 cont. (page 3)
13. Significant date/period: 1986-2015	16. Builder/contractor: n/a	19. On National Register? ☐ individual ☐ district

MISSOURI DEPARTMENT OF NATURAL RESOURCES
STATE HISTORIC PRESERVATION OFFICE, P.O. Box 176,
Jefferson City, MO 65102

ARCHITECTURAL/HISTORIC INVENTORY FORM

		Cite nomination name in box 22 cont. (page 3)
14. Area(s) of significance: AGRICULTURE; SOCIAL HISTORY	17. Original or significant owner: Donald and Carolyn Carver	20. National Register eligible? ☐ individually eligible ☐ district potential ☐ not eligible ☒ not determined
21. History and significance on continuation page. ☒	22. Sources of information on continuation page. ☒	

ARCHITECTURAL INFORMATION

23. Category of property: ☐ building(s) ☒ site ☐ structure ☐ object	30: Roof material: Asphalt shingle	37. Windows: ☐ historic ☒ replacement Pane arrangement: Double Pane/Storm
24. Vernacular or property type: Corner lot, acreage, ponds	31. Chimney placement: Rear slope	38. Acreage (rural): 3 acres Visible from public road? ☒
25. Architectural Style: Raised Ranch style	32. Structural system: Wood siding, board/batten	39. Changes (describe in box 41 cont.): ☐ Addition(s) Date(s):
26. Plan shape: Rectangular	33. Exterior wall cladding: Stone and lumber	☐ Altered Date(s): ☐ Moved Date(s):
27. No. of stories: 1 Front 2	34. Foundation material: Basement	☐Other Date(s): Endangered by: the accumulation of dust, which is to say the way time has a harvest season
28. No. of bays (1st floor): Eight	35. Basement type: Full/finished	40. No. of outbuildings (describe in box 40 cont.): Two
29. Roof type: Medium hip	36. Front porch type/placement: Verandah Partial width	41. Further description of building features and associated resources on continuation page. ☒

MISSOURI DEPARTMENT OF NATURAL RESOURCES
STATE HISTORIC PRESERVATION OFFICE, P.O. Box 176,
Jefferson City, MO 65102

ARCHITECTURAL/HISTORIC INVENTORY FORM

OTHER

42. Current owner/address: [Redacted]	43.Form prepared by (name and org.):	44. Survey date: 2018
	Someone who will not dream of what they could have done with this land. The things grown. The life tilled & nurtured. If only they could. If only.	45. Date of revisions:

FOR SHPO USE

Date entered in inventory:	Level of survey ☐ reconnaissance ☒ intensive	Additional research needed? ☒ yes ☐ no
National Register Status: ☐ listed ☐ in listed district Name: ☐ pending listing ☐ eligible (individually) ☐ eligible (district) ☐ not eligible ☒ not determined	Other:	

MISSOURI DEPARTMENT OF NATURAL RESOURCES
STATE HISTORIC PRESERVATION OFFICE, P.O. Box 176,
Jefferson City, MO 65102

ARCHITECTURAL/HISTORIC INVENTORY FORM

LOCATION MAP (include north arrow)   **LOCATION PHOTOGRAPH**
(taken Oct. 2013)

PHOTOGRAPH

Photographer:	Date:	Description:
RE/MAX Area Real Estate	Dec. 2016	Just out of frame: the pond sheathed by cattails, no longer stocked with crappie. Just out of frame: where the white wooden fence used to be. Just out of frame: the

ARCHITECTURAL/HISTORIC INVENTORY FORM

		apple trees, fruits dangling near where the pen for the bird dogs used to be, by where the tractor used to be. Just within the frame: you can see it—the black walnut tree where girl tried to be where me used to be.

ADDITIONAL INFORMATION:

21. (cont.) History and significance.	Expand box as necessary, or add continuation pages. .
This would be the easy image: my grandpa, in his garage,	This would be the harder image: I was fully listening to my grandpa, and I still think of the smell
showing me how to properly fill & case a shotgun shell	gunpowder and polished copper, the weight of the crank turning over, compressing the shell.
while, half-listening, I stare at the jug of sun	I know that singed carbon breath of a Winchester .243's exhale.
tea my grandma has brewing on the stoop over by the birdbath.	I know the texture of antler bark how much grip it takes to lift a lifeless head
How binary. How romanticizing domestic labor yearning my femininity.	I know how, even among the dried leaves & iron-slicked soil, field-dressing a buck somehow smells like soft old milk
How dismissing generational forms of masculine knowledge passed down.	& I miss it sometimes. A grounding clarity.

MISSOURI DEPARTMENT OF NATURAL RESOURCES
STATE HISTORIC PRESERVATION OFFICE, P.O. Box 176,
Jefferson City, MO 65102

ARCHITECTURAL/HISTORIC INVENTORY FORM

40. (cont.) Description of environment and outbuildings. Expand box as necessary, or add continuation pages.

It used to be quite the imposing fortress—painted all black with red accent trim; the front porch buttressed with storm-sky stone walls. After my parents divorced, my mom's parents softened things up, opting for a sky blue color that remains to this day. But growing up it was a warning. The basement too was black and red. Bright red shag carpet & wooden walls stained soot. A full black bar, black stools. Red glass vases and candle holders. The old rotary dial tv collecting as much dust as my grandma's collection of miniature white porcelain cats starkly posed around the black stone fireplace. The sitting room upstairs was no less intimidating despite its white carpet and blue walls. That same black stone load baring wall up here featured a large black velvet painting of a ship at sea being tossed around on a stormy night. The ceiling was vaulted with dark batten and beam. I felt safe here. I felt protected in this lair, in this hull. I felt comforted as a child by depictions of vampires, necromancy, the dark arts, villains plotting their plots. When you are confronted with a monster, after all, you learn to fight fire with fire.

41. (cont.) Description of primary resource. Expand box as necessary, or add continuation pages.

I'm thinking about if I wasn't the boy in the garage, or the latent girl, but the shell. & what if I was really the sun tea, steeping. & what if it is a spectrum anyway—either way a thing filled, either way a thing warmed through. & how I tried to hold gender distinct from rural knowledge but I was wrong. Gender is agrarian—seeds planted, harvested. We cultivate it. The only real gender binary is you either come into yours fast or slow.

DONALD JUDD'S *UNTITLED (STACK, COR-TEN)*
KUKJE GALLERY
SEOUL, SOUTH KOREA

Look at what's reflecting. Nothing is reflecting off of matte umber, russet surface, rusty purpose. My love, when you started to spend years next to my body, when you saw the men I came from, did you look at our bodies and see accelerated corrosion?

Donald, late in your career you took to using Cor-Ten steel instead of more perfect metals. Sometimes called "weathering steel," you were drawn to its rapid oxidation, its quick patina. Rushed rust.

My love, you only know my dad's damaged body, his chronic porosity. Having witnessed his weathering, I can appreciate the many hues of his sobriety. He's been sober for a decade and a half and we're almost honest with each other. You know, too, my weathered body, my love. Its oil-damp roughness before I finally broke open, a woman, inviting you in. Sometimes I think my gender is mostly a filter, removing my dad by reverse osmosis. But sometimes I think I still have some of his resiliency and maybe I'm better off for it.

This is the last of your stacks, the abrupt series finale, and when I first saw a picture of it I drew an ochre breath, sharp, and wept in place. I've spent so much time with you & your works, feeling disappointed and feeling like my own artistic shortcomings will, like yours did, gurgle up to the surface. And while few artists built as grand a pagoda around their own practice in the way you did with Marfa, I've been fearing that the Midwest will eat at me from the inside, like it did for you, ferric. But this stack, this Cor-Ten column, reminds me of why I sought you in the first place.

Not a stack of shelves but of open boxes, inviting their acrylic color out to the viewer. Green on top of yellow on top of purple on top of ivory on top of orange on top of black. Each color letting the viewer in, closer, closer. I am moved by your gesture to interiority, Donald. Your recognition at last that the body is not perfect, that time breaks apart our particles with a grim consistency. Your recognition that we have a glossy vibrancy to us regardless.

And again, all I see is symbol. Am I too eager to see my dad, my town, redeemed? What else does it say that I'm moved by a conformity of Cor-Ten? Last time I looked at one of your stacks in person I thought about how I am made to feel like a monster for being trans. If I'm being honest with myself, monstrosity is just a mirror form of whiteness. White trans people often feel our monstrosity when being cast out, exiled, kept from seats of power or participation. Monstrosity can be theorized as a mutation or aberration of the "normal" human figure. But Blackness can't be cast out or exiled from a space it was denied access to in the first place. When I feel like a monster, it's just my entitlement quickly mutating, still there, oxidizing in front of everyone's eyes.

RELIEF SPRING

"We can cure Cancer and other tumors without the use of knife. By our methods Cancers are removed without leaving a scar and they never return."-the Bauserman Cancer Cure Sanitarium, Excelsior Springs, 1900

"It is neither scientific nor attractive to medical men to advertise a water as 'curative of stomach diseases; of kidney diseases; of blood diseases.'... if a water Is advertised to cure 'stomach diseases,' it should cure all pathological conditions of the stomach, including cancer of the stomach, etc. Just what we are to understand by 'blood diseases' I am by no means certain."- a letter filed by the Chicago Clinic and Pure Water Journal to Charles Fish, manager of the Excelsior Springs Bottling Company, 1906

The question wasn't whether or not the mineral waters of Excelsior Springs could cure a person of illness but whether or not the town could afford a negative answer. There were costs involved. Infrastructure & advertisements, reputations & investments. The population was growing. The spas were turning into clinics were turning into admittance sanitariums. The bottling company won gold at the 1893 & 1904 World's Fair for their Regent Spring water as well as their Soterian Ginger Ale. The question isn't whether or not the town's business interests had any warning that the end was coming but whether or not they could afford to heed it.

You could close your well or your spa, but someone else would replace you. Like when Relief Spring was closed down & the folks who re-opened it a few years later—investors from Kansas City, a reverend, a professor, and a doctor—built the Salax Spring and Relief Spring Pavilion. There was too much money in the waters. That's the thing about stories in the Midwest: you sink your whole life into the fiction to make a foundation for it. So to compete with the well down the street you start claiming that the water on your site can cure an increasing number of medical vagaries. You start printing ads that position your water as a cure for terminal illnesses and chronic pain. And when folks outside the bubble warn you, you put that letter in a drawer and you carry on.

Excelsior Springs attracted more and more visitors at the same time that the "clean living movement" was appealing itself to American whiteness. Cleanliness being a moral state. Some of the same doctors and scientists extolling the moral and physical virtues of vegetarianism or water treatments or abstinence from masturbation (John Harvey Kellogg, the Carnegie Institution, etc.) were also crafting new forms of race science, like phrenology, to justify white supremacy. There's no separating the clean living movement from the eugenics movement. They are springs that share the same aquifer: *purity.*

All commercial waters in Excelsior Springs began to not only be categorized by mineral composition, but tested for mineral purity. How many milligrams of each mineral. How many ounces of the virginal spring. How many bottles to buy before you're clean. How much to drink to keep yourself white.

These waters are ancient treatments, and they are effective. This town could have been a place of healing, just as it once was a place of healing long before it was a town. White settlers sunk their whole lives into the fiction that they discovered these waters. And in their genocide of the Sac and Fox Nation and the Missouria and the Osage that their fiction required, they never learned how to use the waters. They learned these springs as sites of extraction, not renewal. They really just learned how to turn water into coin; a parlor trick with an inevitable expiration.

In 1963, journalist Ralph Lee Smith wrote a story for the *Saturday Evening Post* titled "The Hucksters of Pain." It was an expose of the fraudulent health claims and practices at the Ball Clinic. The article made no comment about the waters. What did Ball Clinic in was its diagnoses of "fibrositis" and its radio wave treatments and alkaline diets and spinal adjustments—pointless treatment techniques discredited by the Arthritis and Rheumatism Foundation—and Ball Clinic closed down within a year of the story's publication, soon to be followed by nearly every single greedy spa and sanitarium in town.

I wonder if the town was able to breathe then. Just for a moment, did Excelsior truly take a deep, relaxed breath? The lie was found out. There was no more money to protect. Nobody had to pretend anymore. When I stopped pretending to be a man my body moved in the ways it was always supposed to. Years of new possibility stretched before me and I walked forward, light of foot. Excelsior Springs had this chance too. The Midwest has the opportunity each and every day to correct itself, and chooses not to. Excelsior's tourism is reliant upon nostalgia. The town puts on an annual festival called Gatsby Days, in which residents and visitors are encouraged to unironically dress in their Roaring Twenties best & celebrate the days of flourish. Many kids graduating from Excelsior Springs High School have wondered if the town leadership has ever actually read *The Great Gatsby*.

Excelsior Springs has an award-winning, forward-thinking public high school now (if not quite so when I was attending). Excelsior Springs has shops opening up downtown again. Excelsior Springs has a new craft brewery. Excelsior Springs has its own coffee roaster and The Elms Hotel has new ownership and *The Excelsior Springs Standard* is a superb newspaper and the town has some engaged residents working on revitalization and community involvement. But I'm still uneasy when I come back to visit my dad or come back for a funeral or a wedding. The town's economy might be moving forward but its exclusionary cultural and political values—the rank bigotry—are thriving. And there's a growing sense that Excelsior's particular history of settler colonialism, racism, fiction, and fraud are, well, funny. A joke to profit from. The new craft brewery is named "Dubious Claims Brewing Company."

The people of Marfa, of Presidio County, of the Chihuahuan Desert, of the Chinati Mountains, of Pinto Canyon, in the Big Bend of the Rio Grande, will tell you like they told me: the water caught up to you, Donald, and it scares me, the thought of it coming for me too. I think Excelsior Springs might have killed you in the end and to understand why necessitates an understanding of space.

Fifteen concrete structures of identical dimension—2.5 x 2.5 x 5 meters—all hollowed out differently. Some frame the horizon with a curatorial eye, some are windows into the enveloped dark of a closed-off slab. Some are placed in threes, their cave mouths facing each other. Others are boxes, staggered. Visitors can stand on a small hill nearby and watch the shadows waltz over the course of hours. Ever your surly self, you denied the importance of that dance, writing "The concrete boxes are not about shadows but about the possibilities of configurations using these measurements. Most people think it is about shadows. That is what most see. If you don't understand the art, there was no purpose in trying to explain it to you." No matter your mathematical intent, what keeps people in awe of this piece, what you succeeded in, Donald, was to fill the space of the desert with selective shade. Every day, every hour, is charged with new feeling. The place where art activates is the negative space you made. And I don't believe that you wouldn't want that known. After all, what is a shadow if not a legacy?

Donald, you wrote that "The art and architecture of the past that we know is that which remains. The best is that which remains where it was painted, placed or built. Most of the art of the past that could be moved was taken by conquerors. Almost all recent art is conquered as soon as it's made" and *there*, right there, is the Excelsior in you I've been looking for. Your critique of conquest conquered by your colonial ambition. Your project in Marfa was to make art that was unconquerable, an endless installation. This goal required control of the land, and so you became a conqueror to obtain it.

You purchased over 40,000 acres across Pinto Canyon, where you built three ranches—Casa Perez, Casa Morales, and your weekend home, your place of burial, Las Casas—and otherwise kept the rest of the land undeveloped and undisturbed, even refusing to rent cattle grazing rights to ranchers. I think you saw this as conservationism but really it was paternalism, saviorism. Did you even consult with descendents of La Juntan peoples before buying up all that land? All the people that still live on either side of the border, the Julimes and Conchos and Jumanos whose families never left? Did you speak with any Apache people, whose grandfathers and great-grandfathers battled the colonizing United States army around the Chinati Mountains? To see what conservation would have meant for them? It's said that your library has over 150 books about indigenous American peoples and culture, and it seems like that's where you thought their place was: shelved, stored, history. Your need to frame all this tremendous space, your need to control how it's seen, is the Excelsior in you, the Midwest in you, the American in you.

In 1990 you purchased the land rights to the Chinati Hot Springs, a place of healing used by indigenous peoples for centuries. This was a communal place of celebration. This was a place in the desert where people got their drinking water or bathing water or water to wash clothes. And you closed the springs to the public. You put up a gate and a fence and you hired people to stay on the property and guard it. The springs were, in terms of desert distance, not that far from Las Casas, your primary ranch, but people say you rarely used the springs yourself.

You died in 1994. Sixty-five years old. You'd felt a disturbance in your midsection, sick for a bit, but your doctor in Marfa missed the shadow on the CT scan and diagnosed you with a stomach bug that would go away on its own. It didn't, and by the time you sought a second opinion, abroad in Europe for an exhibition, your lymphoma had metastasized. You went for treatment in New York City (where you still owned a cast iron building on Spring Street, gorgeous, if decaying at the time), and that's where you died, three months later, only able to return to Marfa upon your burial.

Many people who were around Marfa at the time still talk about your death as a kind of justice, Donald. I know: I'm writing to a ghost—you either know this or you don't, either way I can't really tell you how people thought you were cursed for keeping the Chinati springs for yourself. Some say you were hexed by an individual spell, others say the land found a way to liberate itself from you.

I say: maybe Excelsior Springs was the curse. Maybe you were doomed, maybe I'm doomed, to see water as a thing to be owned, conquered. I say: no, I don't believe in original sin and even if I did I transitioned out of one kind of it. But I have to admit the viability of the curse, Donald, which came on vicissitudinal, like a sudden, polluted spring. As your lymphoma metastasized, the empty spaces between your chest and the lining of your lungs filled with fluid, as is common, a pleural effusion. Not so much dust to dust as thirst to thirst: you came from a Missouri town of colonized currents, put the spring water of West Texas in a private box, and, in the end, you drowned.

ACCOUNTABILITY

There isn't really a Prada store in Marfa. It's a false Prada storefront, an art installation from 2005, a theatrical set piece in desert sun floodlight. I've spent enough time recognizing limitations to see the problem: it's a work of art trying to critique the changes to Marfa—the flow of culture and capital—that were brought along by art itself, by what continued after you passed. Thank you for showing me your limitations, Donald, and helping me see my own in the negative space between my questions. What fills the spaces isn't whether or not I can afford to stay away from the wood smoke and crappie and dogwood blossoms of Excelsior but whether I can find home in people and not in stolen land. What fills the spaces isn't whether or not I can forgive my father (I have) but whether or not I can let go of the concepts of heredity and family. There are costs involved. What fills the empty spaces isn't whether or not the laborers of Marfa can afford designer clothing but whether or not they can weather all the change. It's only getting hotter, drier. The border police flourish, casting their own shadows. This is about liquidity. Material resources amassed by the wealthy, stacked. What fills the spaces isn't whether or not art can ever be its own object, set apart from precariat narrative, but whether or not we can afford the attempt. Objectivity is a whiteness is a hollowing out of a place is a dubious claim to the essential. That's all whiteness can ever be: an empty aquifer—violent and permeable—waiting for its own erosion, for flood, revolution. And maybe my dad was right when he saw me for the first time after I transitioned and said "my son is gone, he's really gone." Maybe I am only my own daughter or maybe I am the daughter of so many people and maybe the two of us can only heal if we see each other for who we are and not for the family roles we both failed to fit. What fills the spaces isn't blood, being thicker, but what we all have in common, what each of us shares. How much of us is made of water.

HALL OF WATERS

A lot of my research & historical facts about Excelsior Springs, MO came from Missouri historical site survey forms commissioned by the city of Excelsior Springs. I source a lot of information from a 2011-2012 series of surveys conducted by Dean Wolfenbarger, of a Colorado-based company called Three Gables Preservation, as well as a 1991 series of surveys & a 1994 landscape survey, also conducted by Wolfenbarger, when his company was based in Kansas City. My time spent reading these public record Missouri state forms were also the direct inspiration behind the two historical site survey hermit crab essays in this book. I learned from many sources local to Excelsior Springs as well, including the Excelsior Springs Museum and Archive; and local historians Sonya and Kevin Morgan, & their websites theidlehour.com and fishingriver.com. And of course, Excelsior Springs being my hometown, there was plenty of experiential knowledge derived from my life & the lives of people I know.

My writing on Donald Judd should not be constituted as a complete depiction of the person or the art he made. I have no formal training in art criticism, and there is so much of his complicated biography & politics that is left out of this book. That said, my artistic pursuit of connection with Judd and the critique that came of it was extensively researched. I read all of "Donald Judd Writings" (2016, David Zwimmer Books), edited by Flavin Judd and Caitlin Murray, which is a compilation of essentially every published article Donald Judd ever wrote, as well as previously-unpublished notes & journals. The Judd Foundation and the Chinati Foundation make plenty of information about Judd and Marfa available, of course. I also spoke with people connected to Marfa about Judd. Being an essential artist, Judd had plenty of articles written about him & his work in newspapers and magazines across the world, many of which I read during the time I wrote this book. Very special mention belongs to David Keller, whose article, "Taming the Healing Waters: The History of the Chinati Hot Springs," from the second quarter 2012 issue of Cenzio (a journal of far West Texas arts and culture), confirmed what I was being told from people connected to Marfa about Judd purchasing the springs & closing off access to them. Other sources of special mention include Josh T Franco's letter to Judd published in fluentcollab.org; the site texasbeyondhistory.

net for information about the indigenous La Juntan peoples of Pinto Canyon; and a mysterious art resource site with no direct homepage run by user "Solfrian2" on the seattleclouds.com app hosting service, particularly for Solfrian2's history and GPS data for Judd's rural houses, Casa Morales, Casa Perez, and Las Casas.

BIBLIOGRAPHY

This work has engaged with countless pieces of media, text, visual art, and other resources. Some of those most explicitly used in researching this piece are as follows:

American Italian Pasta Company. "Annual Report 2002." http://media.corporate-ir.net/media_files/NYS/PLB/reports/2002arl.pdf

Baumgardner, Julie. "Judd's Late Cor-Ten Works: Evolutionary or Unchanging?" Art In America. Dec. 17, 2015. https://www.artinamericamagazine.com/news-features/news/juddrsquos-late-cor-ten-works-evolutionary-or-unchanging/

The Chinati Foundation, various resources. Chinati.org

Lynne Cooke, Liam Gillick, Mark Godfrey, Mary Heilmann, James Meyer, Jasper Morrison, David Musgrave, Deyan Sudjic and Richard Wentworth, "What Is the Object?" Frieze. Issue 82, April 2004

Donald Judd Furniture, "Library Bed 15." https://judd.furniture/product/library-bed-15/?attribute_pa_materials-wood=common-pine

Downtown Excelsior Partnership. "Mineral Water History Walking Tour of Excelsior Springs." https://visitexcelsior.com/maps/WellWalkingTour.pdf

Ennis, Michael. "The Minimalist." Texas Monthly. April 2003

Environmental Protection Agency. "Pasta Manufacturing." https://www3.epa.gov/ttnchie1/ap42/ch09/final/c9s09-5.pdf

Excelsior Springs Museum and Archive, various records and advertising materials.

Fenton, Laura. "The Rise of Marfa." Curbed. https://www.curbed.com/2014/10/22/10033194/marfa-texas-donald-judd-interior-design-modernism

Franco, Josh. "Long Read: Letter to Donald Judd." Fluent Collab. Issue 196, Sept. 14, 2012. http://www.fluentcollab.org/mbg/index.php/interview/index/196/135

Judd, Donald. Donald Judd Writings. David Zwimmer Books, 2016. Eds. Flavin Judd and Caitlin Murray

The Judd Foundation, various resources. Juddfoundation.org

Judd, Rainer. Marfa Voices. The Judd Foundation Oral History Project. 2007, film (25 minutes)

Keller, David. "Taming the Healing Waters: The History of the Chinati Hot Springs." Cenzio Journal. Second Quarter 2012

Kennedy, Randy. "Donald Judd, Artist, Revealed as a Philosopher-Critic by His Children." The New York Times. Dec. 25, 2016

Kilgore, Samantha. "Excelsior Springs Gives State of the City." The Excelsior Springs Standard, March 30, 2018

MacCormack, John. "72 Hours or Less: Chinati Hot Springs." My San Antonio. June 10, 2002. https://www.mysanantonio.com/life/travel/article/72-Hours-or-Less-Chinati-Hot-Springs-3617186.php

Mayo, C.M. "A Spell at Chinati Hot Springs." C.M. Mayo's Podcasting Project—Marfa Mondays. Episode 8, Nov. 04, 2012. Podcast (27 minutes). Guest: Diana Burbach

McCleary, A.S. The Legend of Peace Valley, Told by Wapoo, Keeper of the Springs. The McCleary Sanitarium and Clinic, Excelsior Springs, MO. 1940.

Messina, John. "Principle and Practice: The Ethic and Efficacy of Donald Judd's Interventions at La Mansana de Chinati." 98th ACSA Annual Meeting—Re.Building. Association of Collegiate Schools of Architecture. 2010

Morgan, Sonya. Theidlehour.com

Morgan, Kevin. Fishingriver.com/archaic

Perrottet, Tony. "Donald Judd's Private Retreat." Wall Street Journal Magazine. March 29, 2017.https://www.wsj.com/articles/donald-judds-private-retreat-1490792313

Reike, Lauren. Rosin Preservation LLC. Survey CL-AS-015, Boardinghouse Historic Resource Inventory. 2014. Missouri Department of Natural Resources, State Historic Preservation Office

Sanborn Fire Insurance Maps, 1894-1940. Kansas City, MO Public Library, Missouri Valley Special Collections

Sanders, Samantha. "Why Donald Judd Brought His Art to Marfa, Texas." Artistsnetwork.com. https://www.artistsnetwork.com/magazine/donald-judd/

Smith, Roberta. "Donald Judd: 'Stacks.'" The New York Times. Oct. 24, 2013

Smith, Roberta. "Donald Judd, Leading Minimalist Sculptor, Dies at 65." The New York Times. Feb.13, 1994

Tate Modern. "Donald Judd—Exhibition Guide." https://www.tate.org.uk/whats-on/tate-modern/exhibition/donald-judd/donald-judd-exhibition-guide/donald-judd-exhibition-1

Texas Beyond History. "Part-Time Farmers: Patarabueyes of La Junta." Texas Archeological Research Laboratory at the University of Texas at Austin. https://texasbeyondhistory.net/trans-p/peoples/farmers.html

Texas Beyond History. "La Junta Reconsidered." Texas Archeological Research Laboratory at the University of Texas at Austin. https://texasbeyondhistory.net/junta/reconsidered.html

Waldow, Jennie. "Art in the Landscape: Exploring Marfa, TX." Inside/Out—A MoMA/MoMA PS1 Blog. https://www.moma.org/explore/inside_out/2014/06/30/art-in-the-landscape-exploring-marfa-tx/

Wolfenbarger, Dean. Three Gables Preservation. Survey CL-AS-009, Hall of Waters and Central Place District. 1991. Missouri Department of Natural Resources, State Historic Preservation Office

Wolfenbarger, Dean. Three Gables Preservation. Excelsior Springs Park Driveway System, Landscape Architectural Historic Survey. 1994. Missouri Department of Natural Resources, State Historic Preservation Office

Wolfenbarger, Dean. Three Gables Preservation. Survey CL-AS-010, Mineral Wells and Springs. 2011. Missouri Department of Natural Resources, State Historic Preservation Office

"Casa Morales/Casa Perez." http://seattleclouds.com/myapplications/solfrian2/BLDGapp/morales.html

"Las Casas Ranch." http://seattleclouds.com/myapplications/solfrian2/BLDGapp/ayala.html

ACKNOWLEDGMENTS

So, so many thanks go out to Elæ [Lynne DeSilva-Johnson] and the truly tireless work that they do for The Operating System and for the literary world as a whole. Thank you to the many-splendored talents that collectively contribute to the making of The Operating System. I'm so grateful that this book found its home with y'all.

Thank you to the editors who worked with me in shaping and publishing early work from this project: Colette Arrand & Raquel Salas Rivera (*The Wanderer*), Gina Myers & Gabriella Torres (*the tiny*), Lindsay Lusby & Emma Sovich (*Cherry Tree*), Andrew Cartwright (*phoebe*), Sherri Caudell (*Shock of the Femme*), Andrew Sargus Klein (*Territory*), Callum Angus (*smoke + mold*), Silas Hansen (*Waxwing*), Ander Monson, Katie Jean Shinkle, & Nicole Walker, & T Clutch Fleischmann (*DIAGRAM*), and Blake Butler & Sarah Rose Etter (*The Fanzine*).

There are many, many good people from or living in or connected to Excelsior Springs that held space for me throughout my childhood and still do today. Too many to make a complete list, though I must thank Josh Nall & Katie Lee, Derek Mueller, Patrick & Vicki & Mark Rippeto, Nicholas Whitehead, Halliday Bertram, Jesse Jamison, Ben Troutman, Sonny Uftring, Erik Holtzclaw, Andrea Hamachek, Megan Teeter, Nikki Rogers, Nathan & Liz Bettendorf Bowman, Cathy Clevenger Minton, Christen Everett, Jerilyn Griffin, Lauren Cazzell, Rachel Lane, my dad (Doug), my brother (Bret), and my Aunt Rhonda, among others.

I wouldn't be who I am today without the influence of Rebecca Browning. You taught me more than you could ever know about how to be a woman in the arts, about how to be an artist.

My everlasting thanks go out to my cohort and faculty & mentors in the MFA program in creative writing & the English Department at The University of Alabama. Thank you all for holding me dear. Thanks in particular to Michael Martone, Dave Madden, Brian Oliu, Katie Berger, Freya Gibbon, Abbas Abidi, Jason McCall, Laura Kochman, Annie Agnone, Brandi Wells, Zach Doss (RIP),

Leia Penina Wilson, Colin Rafferty, Elizabeth Wade, Yolanda Manora, Katie Jean Shinkle, Jenny Gropp, Emily Wittman, Tasha Coryell, Jonathan Dubow, Krystin Gollihue, Kori Hensell, and Emma Sovich for pushing my writing & my thinking forward. Thank you Bob Weatherly and the whole crew at the original Egan's Bar in Tuscaloosa. It was the most powerful idea of home that I've ever experienced. It was the best bar in the world. Thank you, Tuscaloosa.

Thank you to my earliest writing mentors, when I was attending Northwest Missouri State University: John Gallaher, Rebecca Aronson, Bryn Gribben, Roger Kirschbaum (RIP), Bruce Litte (RIP), Jeffrey Loomis. Thank you to my Theater Northwest pals, and my group of English major/minor nerds that let me be my silly self: Jared Bailey, Brett & Cristy Henggeler, Jon Ferguson, Michaela Jordan, Patrick Fedo, Andrea Jones, Liz Iverson, Adam "Ace" Smith, and Amanda Meyer, among others.

Deep gratitude for my fellow editors at *Sundog Lit*: Melissa Wiley, Carrie Chappel, Cynthia Brandon-Slocum, Leela Chantrelle, Jennifer Huang, and former editors Laura Citino & Roy Guzmán. Your patience and kindness with me has been crucial for the life of this book.

Thank you to my chosen family in Philadelphia, too numerous to list here. You know who you are, and you have kept me alive.

I can never express enough appreciation for my wife, my love, Laura Kochman. Every day spent with you is a gift.

Thank you to our cat, Vladimir, who comforted me in his final years as I was writing this book.

Thanks most of all to Connie Carver Grass, my mom. I miss you.

DEMYTHOLOGIZED GROUND

A CONVERSATION WITH BERRY GRASS

Greetings comrade! Thank you for talking to us about your process today!
Can you introduce yourself, in a way that you would choose?

My name is Berry Grass (they/them or she/her). I'm an essayist. I'm a transsexual. I'm a metalhead. I've mostly been a teacher, and I would like to still be one. I grew up in an interesting part of Missouri—Excelsior Spring, MO (which is also the micro-level subject of this book) is pretty much a rural town, but it's substantially developed for its size due to its history as a tourist site, but it's not a suburb of Kansas City, but it's only a half hour's drive away from Kansas City. I also lived for a time in Tuscaloosa, AL, and I've been living in Philadelphia, PA since 2014.

Why do you write?

I think I'm an essayist because I've always felt better about my thinking if I've written through it. I was essentially essaying as a young person just to make proper decisions, and that trait has stuck with me.

When did you decide you were a poet/writer/artist (and/or: do you feel comfortable calling yourself a poet/writer/artist, what other titles or affiliations do you prefer/feel are more accurate)?

I don't know when I decided I'd actually call myself a writer. Maybe when I started publishing? I realize that's a foolheaded way to think, but I remember feeling a difference between "I write" and "I'm a writer"—feelings that I wouldn't necessarily validate now. I did accept the term "essayist" more quickly. There's no implicit status or level of success with "essayist" like there is for "writer." Anyone who calls themselves an essayist probably fully deserves to do so.

What's a "poet" (or "writer" or "artist") anyway?
What do you see as your cultural and social role (in the literary / artistic / creative community and beyond)?

I think the only role that I really want to fill is to be a writer that other trans writers admire. I want to create spaces for trans writers and I want to leverage my experiences and my degrees to boost trans writers. I run an occasional reading series for trans writers in Philadelphia called "Tragic: the Gathering," and I pay each reader upwards of $30, a lot of it coming from my paltry bank account.

Beyond the fulfillment I get from that, my role in the literary community is to be just another essay nerd, writing & appreciating, & talking about essays. Essayists are a friendly bunch. That's my role.

Talk about the process or instinct to move these poems (or your work in general) as independent entities into a body of work. How and why did this happen? Have you had this intention for a while? What encouraged and/or confounded this (or a book, in general) coming together? Was it a struggle? Did you envision this collection as a collection or understand your process as writing or making specifically around a theme while the poems themselves were being written / the work was being made? How or how not?

My intention from the very first draft of the first of these essays I wrote (the titular piece "Hall of Waters") was that I'd be writing at least a short sequence of linked essays & lyric memoirs. I had the idea to write about my mineral water hometown & my experience growing up there through short pieces that were "about" a specific water-related site in Excelsior. Because these former springs or wells or etc had geospecific locations, I could use that area as a jumping off point for my memories. I knew these pieces were not just linked in terms of subject, but also in this approach where specific place within the town was the catalyst for the essaying. In other words, it was the form as well as the subject that was always-already linking the work as I wrote from late 2016 through this year.

What I didn't necessarily expect was that in the course of writing my Excelsior essays, I would stumble onto a second set of linked essays—about the infamous godfather of American minimalist sculpture, Donald Judd. I began to write about a spring close to Judd's parent's house in Excelsior Springs. Judd was born in Excelsior! And as I was writing that piece (which was later scrapped), I realized I had a lot more to say about Judd and *to* Judd. So I began writing essays titled after individual works of his, and with the goal of trying to dialogue with the dead so as to figure out what, if anything, was Excelsior Springs about Donald Judd. What ended up being written was a personal essay form that was simultaneously ekphrastic and epistolary.

Long story short: that I had two different sets of linked essays revolving around the same town (and the U.S. Midwest more broadly) told me that I maybe had a book manuscript going.

What formal structures or other constrictive practices (if any) do you use in the creation of your work? Have certain teachers or instructive environments, or readings/writings/work of other creative people informed the way you work/write?

I do not generally place formal constrictive practices on my writing, particularly when I'm essaying. I feel the responsibility to convey truth of experience and truth of feeling, and to use research truthfully. And I feel the responsibility when essaying to not just follow my digressions of thought but to show those digressions happening. But to me, that is quite the opposite of constrictive, and that is why I love the essay form so much. One structural practice I do tend to use is to whenever possible make sure that the form of an essay reflects the content of the essay. At least in a small way, as in the cases of the Judd essays using ekphrasis for instance. Or in a huge, challenging way—like the "hermit crab" essays that were literally written in the form of Missouri state survey forms for the historical record (shout out to Brenda Miller for coining the term "hermit crab essay" for essays that use borrowed non-literary forms).

My biggest source of perpetual inspiration is the international essayist community. Essayists get so excited & inspired by each other's work, so much so that there's even journals like Assay that exist to help us share essay theory and pedagogy with each other.

Speaking of monikers, what does your title represent? How was it generated? Talk about the way you titled the book, and how your process of naming (individual pieces, sections, etc) influences you and/or colors your work specifically.

As I mentioned before, the first essay from this project that I wrote was "Hall of Waters," which I would eventually title the book after. Perhaps partly because in writing about this one ornate building & its history, I was able to initially ground basically all of the themes of the book. There's no more important water-related site in Excelsior Springs than the Hall of Waters. It's built at the site of the first spring that was discovered by settlers, the spring that is the reason the town exists at all. The building presently hosts city hall and the municipal court. Plus: it just sounds cool. *Hall of Waters*. It sounds almost mythic. It's grandiose. It sounds like a temple in a *Legend of Zelda* game or something. And considering that I want this book to demythologize the town's self-imposed narratives, the title of the book helps to establish that there's myth to demythologize in the first place.

The titles of the individual pieces certainly reflect that this is a book about place. Apart from a small handful of pieces (maybe five in the entire book), every piece has a specific place in the title. There's the water springs essays that are titled after specific springs & wells, but even the Judd essays not only have a specific work in the title, but also the city and state or country that the work is installed in. The way these titles operate is to prevent readers from ever forgetting that the thinking & the research in this book is very much tied, inseparably, to a specific place with a specific history of specific people & cultures.

What does this particular work represent to you as indicative of your method/ creative practice? your history? your mission/intentions/hopes/plans?

In a very immediate and obvious sense, this book represents the milestone of having written and published my first book. Its existence is a kind of bulwark against my self-directed negativity and anxiety and imposter syndrome. It's also not lost on me that this book is both 1) my first project since hormonally transitioning, and 2) is a significant departure from the longer 15+ page essays that I tended to write (and my unpublished book-length manuscript of literary journalism that was 200+ pages). So I feel like this book represents to me that I am not stagnating as a writer, and that I have the capacity to change and grow.

What does this book DO (as much as what it says or contains)?

The book says a lot about demythologizing the Midwest—telling truth to the stories that the Midwest likes to tell itself. Telling truth to settler colonialism and whiteness. I hope that the book *does* this in such a way that isn't itself enacting harm. I wanted to write about whiteness in a plain, understated way. There is use of lyricism in this book, but I didn't want to write about settler colonial violence with lyrical language. I didn't want to write in a lyric way about individual moments of anti-Black violence that I observed in my town because that's not my place as a white writer to do. What I hope this book does instead is help uplift & restore the Missouria & the Osage & the Sac and Fox Nation to the record and history of Excelsior Springs and its waters. I hope that the book can help uplift and restore Travis Mellion and Robert Spence and Katie & W.A. Doxey and other Black laborers and skilled water treatment facilitators to Excelsior Springs' history.

Another thing that I hope this book does is attempt to be what a leftist creative nonfiction can be. Readers will be the judge of whether this book is on the right track, but what I wanted to do was ground the essay (and its individual narrator and its lyric I) in a collective experience, or in a history of collective experiences. Nothing about my experiences as a trans woman are unique to me. Nothing about the settler colonialism & white supremacy of Excelsior Springs is unique to Excelsior Springs. I want this book to take a micro-level look at my life and experiences in this town so as to be able to speak broadly to how the Midwest creates and replicates the conditions that occupy indigenous land, oppress BIPOC, castigate queerness, etc.

What would be the best possible outcome for this book? What might it do in the world, and how will its presence as an object facilitate your creative role in your community and beyond? What are your hopes for this book, and for your practice?

My pie-in-the-sky goal would be for this book to inspire other settlers in the U.S. to examine the real histories of the places where they grew up, to inspire other settlers to at least recognize themselves as settlers. What are the fictions that reify power where you are from? What is the narrative behind the given narrative? Who is being erased? I do hope that readers will seek out these questions for the places that their lives take shape in. Additionally, I would love it if any trans reader, particularly a rural trans reader, sees a bit of themselves in this book. Its existence as a print object will help get this into libraries and hopefully onto course syllabi.

And honestly? I look forward to print copies getting a little water stained and yellowed and mildewed with time. That feels right for this book.

Let's talk a little bit about the role of poetics and creative community in social and political activism, so present in our daily lives as we face the often sobering, sometimes dangerous realities of the Capitalocene. How does your process, practice, or work otherwise interface with these conditions?

I'm not sure that it completely does. I feel like there's certainly a role that literary writing plays in not only offering critique of the ravages of capital & colonization, but even more crucially in expanding our imaginations of what is possible to fight for and achieve and implement. Poetry and fiction seem better positioned to work on imagination than nonfiction. So mostly I leave whatever political organizing I do (& won't speak directly about online) to exist separate from my writing. But as I said, I am interested in building out what a leftist/collectivist/anti-capital essaying can look like for me or for others. So we'll see.

Is there anything else we should have asked, or that you want to share?

I suppose that I just want to say that Donald Judd is a more complex figure than he's perhaps characterized in this book. I wanted (and I think the desperation behind this want is evident in the narrator-self as the book proceeds) to figure out what negativity from Excelsior Springs did Judd carry with him through life, as a way of protecting myself. A way of divining the future from looking into the past, I guess. So this book is critical of Judd's shortcomings. And he had PLENTY—I should know, I read all of his collected published writings and journals (so many opinions about architecture!). A...complicated political mind; he was deeply anti-war, and probably considered himself a leftist (though he comes off in his journals as almost a radical centrist, with the anti-Communist takes and what with the houses in Texas, New York City, and Switzerland, and his paternalistic deployment of his wealth). And he was a great artist. I don't want that to get lost amidst my critique. Instead of dismissing him for his shortcomings & flaws, I kept returning to his work and his thought, kept reaching for what I thought he could teach me.

ABOUT THE AUTHOR

Berry Grass has lived in rural Missouri, Tuscaloosa, & now Philadelphia. Their essays & poems appear in *DIAGRAM, The Normal School, Barrelhouse, Sonora Review, BOAAT,* and *The Wanderer,* among other publications. They are a 2019 nominee for the Krause Essay Prize. Their chapbook, *Collector's Item,* was published in 2014 by Corgi Snorkel Press. They recieved their MFA from the University of Alabama, where they served as Nonfiction Editor of *Black Warrior Review.* They curate "Tragic: the Gathering," an occasional transgender reading series in South Philly. When they aren't presently reading submissions as Nonfiction Editor of *Sundog Lit,* they are embodying what happens when a Virgo watches too much professional wrestling. Follow at @thebgrass on Twitter, @berry. grass on Instagram.

The Operating System uses the language "print document" to differentiate from the book-object as part of our mission to distinguish the act of documentation-in-book-FORM from the act of publishing as a backwards-facing replication of the book's agentive *role* as it may have appeared the last several centuries of its history. Ultimately, I approach the book as TECHNOLOGY: one of a variety of printed documents (in this case, bound) that humans have invented and in turn used to archive and disseminate ideas, beliefs, stories, and other evidence of production.

Ownership and use of printing presses and access to (or restriction of printed materials) has long been a site of struggle, related in many ways to revolutionary activity and the fight for civil rights and free speech all over the world. While (in many countries) the contemporary quotidian landscape has indeed drastically shifted in its access to platforms for sharing information and in the widespread ability to "publish" digitally, even with extremely limited resources, the importance of publication on physical media has not diminished. In fact, this may be the most critical time in recent history for activist groups, artists, and others to insist upon learning, establishing, and encouraging personal and community documentation practices. Hear me out.

With The OS's print endeavors I wanted to open up a conversation about this: the ultimately radical, transgressive act of creating PRINT /DOCUMENTATION in the digital age. It's a question of the archive, and of history: who gets to tell the story, and what evidence of our life, our behaviors, our experiences are we leaving behind? We can know little to nothing about the future into which we're leaving an unprecedentedly digital document trail — but we can be assured that publications, government agencies, museums, schools, and other institutional powers that be will continue to leave BOTH a digital and print version of their production for the official record. Will we?

As a (rogue) anthropologist and long time academic, I can easily pull up many accounts about how lives, behaviors, experiences — how THE STORY of a time or place — was pieced together using the deep study of correspondence, notebooks, and other physical documents which are no longer the norm in many lives and practices. As we move our creative behaviors towards digital note taking, and even audio and video, what can we predict about future technology that is in any way assuring that our stories will be accurately told – or told at all? How will we leave these things for the record?

In these documents we say:
WE WERE HERE, WE EXISTED, WE HAVE A DIFFERENT STORY

- Elæ [Lynne DeSilva-Johnson], Founder/Creative Director
THE OPERATING SYSTEM, Brooklyn NY 2018

RECENT & FORTHCOMING FULL LENGTH
OS PRINT::DOCUMENTS and PROJECTS, 2018-19

2019

Y - Lori Anderson Moseman
Ark Hive-Marthe Reed
I Made for You a New Machine and All it Does is Hope - Richard Lucyshyn
Illusory Borders-Heidi Reszies
A Year of Misreading the Wildcats - Orchid Tierney
Collaborative Precarity Bodyhacking Work-book and Research Guide - stormy
budwig, Elae [Lynne DeSilva-Johnson] and Cory Tamler
We Are Never The Victims - Timothy DuWhite
Of Color: Poets' Ways of Making | An Anthology of Essays on Transformative Poetics
-Amanda Galvan Huynh & Luisa A. Igloria, Editors
The Suitcase Tree - Filip Marinovich
In Corpore Sano: Creative Practice and the Challenged* Body - Elae [Lynne DeSilva-
Johnson] and Amanda Glassman, Editors

KIN(D)* TEXTS AND PROJECTS

A Bony Framework for the Tangible Universe-D. Allen
Opera on TV-James Lowell Brunton
Hall of Waters-Berry Grass
Transitional Object-Adrian Silbernagel

GLOSSARIUM: UNSILENCED TEXTS AND TRANSLATIONS

Śnienie / Dreaming - Marta Zelwan, (Poland, trans. Victoria Miluch)
Alparegho: Pareil-À-Rien / Alparegho, Like Nothing Else - Hélène Sanguinetti
(France, trans. Ann Cefola)
High Tide Of The Eyes - Bijan Elahi (Farsi-English/dual-language)
trans. Rebecca Ruth Gould and Kayvan Tahmasebian
In the Drying Shed of Souls: Poetry from Cuba's Generation Zero
Katherine Hedeen and Víctor Rodríguez Núñez, translators/editors
Street Gloss - Brent Armendinger with translations for Alejandro Méndez, Mercedes
Roffé, Fabián Casas, Diana Bellessi, and Néstor Perlongher (Argentina)
Operation on a Malignant Body - Sergio Loo (Mexico, trans. Will Stockton)
Are There Copper Pipes in Heaven - Katrin Ottarsdóttir
(Faroe Islands, trans. Matthew Landrum)

An Absence So Great and Spontaneous It Is Evidence of Light - Anne Gorrick
The Book of Everyday Instruction - Chloë Bass
Executive Orders Vol. II - a collaboration with the Organism for Poetic Research
One More Revolution - Andrea Mazzariello
Chlorosis - Michael Flatt and Derrick Mund
Sussuros a Mi Padre - Erick Sáenz
Abandoners - Lesley Ann Wheeler
Jazzercise is a Language - Gabriel Ojeda-Sague
Born Again - Ivy Johnson
Attendance - Rocío Carlos and Rachel McLeod Kaminer
Singing for Nothing - Wally Swist
Walking Away From Explosions in Slow Motion - Gregory Crosby
Field Guide to Autobiography - Melissa Eleftherion

KIN(D)* TEXTS AND PROJECTS

Sharing Plastic - Blake Nemec
The Ways of the Monster - Jay Besemer

GLOSSARIUM: UNSILENCED TEXTS AND TRANSLATIONS

The Book of Sounds - Mehdi Navid (Farsi dual language, trans. Tina Rahimi
Kawsay: The Flame of the Jungle - María Vázquez Valdez (Mexico, trans. Margaret Randall)
Return Trip / Viaje Al Regreso - Israel Dominguez; (Cuba, trans. Margaret Randall)

for our full catalog please visit:
https://squareup.com/store/the-operating-system/

deeply discounted Book of the Month and Chapbook Series subscriptions
are a great way to support the OS's projects and publications!
sign up at: http://www.theoperatingsystem.org/subscribe-join/

DOC U MENT
/däkyəmənt/

First meant "instruction" or "evidence," whether written or not.

noun - a piece of written, printed, or electronic matter that provides information or evidence or that serves as an official record
verb - record (something) in written, photographic, or other form
synonyms - paper - deed - record - writing - act - instrument

[*Middle English, precept, from Old French, from Latin documentum, example, proof, from docre, to teach; see dek- in Indo-European roots.*]

Who is responsible for the manufacture of value?

Based on what supercilious ontology have we landed in a space where we vie against other creative people in vain pursuit of the fleeting credibilities of the scarcity economy, rather than freely collaborating and sharing openly with each other in ecstatic celebration of MAKING?

While we understand and acknowledge the economic pressures and fear-mongering that threatens to dominate and crush the creative impulse, we also believe that
now more than ever we have the tools to relinquish agency via cooperative means,
fueled by the fires of the Open Source Movement.

Looking out across the invisible vistas of that rhizomatic parallel country
we can begin to see our community beyond constraints, in the place
where intention meets resilient, proactive, collaborative organization.

Here is a document born of that belief, sown purely of imagination and will.
When we document we assert. We print to make real, to reify our being there.
When we do so with mindful intention to address our process, to open our work
to others, to create beauty in words in space, to respect and acknowledge the strength
of the page we now hold physical, a thing in our hand, we remind ourselves that,
like Dorothy: *we had the power all along, my dears.*

THE PRINT! DOCUMENT SERIES
is a project of
the trouble with bartleby
in collaboration with
the operating system

CPSIA information can be obtained
at www.ICGtesting.com
Printed in the USA
BVHW030153210819
556404BV00001B/93/P

9 781946 031549